Winning Golf
THE PROFESSIONAL WAY

Winning Golf

THE PROFESSIONAL WAY

Bob Zender
and
Charles B. Cleveland

DODD, MEAD & COMPANY

New York

Library of Congress Cataloging in Publication Data

Zender, Bob.
  Winning golf—the professional way.

  1. Golf.   I. Cleveland, Charles B.   II. Title.
GV965.Z46 1985   796.352'3   84-21172
ISBN 0-396-08368-4

6-16-86 — MW— 36/29

Contents

Introduction
By Andy North

I've seen many golf books over the years, but none has caught my attention quite as quickly as the title of Bob Zender's book, *Winning Golf—The Professional Way.*

Bob and I played the pro tour together for a number of years, and I have a lot of respect for his knowledge of the game. More than once he has spotted something in my game that needed correcting. So I know him not only as a fellow competitor but as a fine student of the game as well.

His book brought back vividly my greatest moment of "winning golf": the pressure putt on the final hole in the 1978 National Open at Cherry Hills Country Club. Many of the lessons that Bob Zender tells about in his book are the lessons I learned—some of them the hard way—in that 1978 National Open.

Cherry Hills is located just outside Denver. Because of the mile-high altitude, you get a lot more distance on your shots. In addition, some critics believe that the front nine at Cherry Hills lacks the distance of a championship course.

But even if you believe that (and I don't), Cherry Hills deserves its first-class reputation. The rough, as you might expect, was toughened up for the Open. If you landed in that four-inch bluegrass, it was almost impossible to control your iron shots.

The fairways were so narrow they demanded pinpoint accuracy off the tee. Temperatures were in the 90's, and the greens were baked hard and fast. There was no room for error anywhere on the course.

But the real test came on the closing holes. There are none tougher anywhere on the tour. It was at this same golf course that Arnold Palmer came from back in the pack on the fourth round with a spectacular display of golf to win the 1960 National Open. It electrified the gallery and, in the years that followed, it became Palmer's trademark to "charge" the closing holes with daring, aggressive golf.

I started out with three excellent rounds of golf—70, 70, and 71; began the final round with four straight one-putt greens; and by the thirteenth hole had a four-stroke lead.

Then trouble started. On the fourteenth I hooked the ball into the deep rough and bogied. On the par-3 fifteenth hole I made the mistake that Bob warns you about. I overshot the green!

The green was elevated and the pin in the front right corner. I hit a 5-iron too far, and the ball rolled off the green into a bunker; it took me two shots to escape and a pair of putts to hole out, and my lead was down to two strokes.

I almost got into trouble on the sixteenth hole when my approach shot landed in a bunker, but I exploded well and saved my par. The seventeenth is a challenging hole; the green is on a small island. I put my approach in the center of the green and holed out in two.

Which brought me to the final hole. From that tee, if you hit left, the ball goes into the lake. A shot to the right is either out of bounds or lands in a terrible rough. Between the two there is only about a fifteen-yard landing area.

I had birdied the eighteenth hole twice earlier, but this time I played it more cautiously. I drove with a 3-iron, but the wind was behind me and the ball carried into the rough.

I used an 8-iron but made another of the mistakes Bob warns about—I left the ball in the rough on the left. Worse, between my ball and the pin was a bunker, and I chose that time to hit

my worst shot of the tournament; it was a poor wedge shot that landed smack in the middle of the bunker.

Thus, I had not only hit two bad shots in a row, but also a third. J. C. Snead and Dave Stockton had already holed out with scores of 286. I had to get down in two from the trap or risk a three-way tie or worse.

This time I made up for my mistake. I hit a fine explosion shot to within four feet of the pin, and I now faced the make-or-break putt. I lined up the putt, but I wasn't comfortable, so I stepped back. I took my stance a second time and again it didn't seem right.

Some people thought I was going through the yippies, and I've got to admit the pressure was on. But as Bob points out, if you have doubts about any putt, stop and wait for your confidence to catch up.

I did, and the ball went right in the middle of the cup. With that putt I became the National Open champion.

It wasn't easy then and it still isn't easy to be a winner at golf. But I am sure that if you follow Bob Zender's advice, you'll play better golf and enjoy it more. And you'll win your share of golf matches.

Winning Golf
THE PROFESSIONAL WAY

Chapter 1

How to Play
Your Best Golf

Possibly the toughest challenge in golf is to qualify for the PGA Tour. It is the only way an amateur can get his "card"—the right to play on the big-money circuit. In 1971, the year I turned pro, 357 players tried out, including three former U.S. Amateur champions, several public links and college title holders, and a few top-flight players from overseas.

How tough was it to break into the pro ranks that year? Numbers tell the story. In most pro tournaments, you have a fifty-fifty chance of staying in the running. Half the players survive the cut and have a shot at some of the prize money. By contrast, the process of qualifying to become a pro is far more demanding.

Thus, while 357 of us started out in the class of 1971, only twenty-three scored well enough to be awarded our cards. Just getting a chance to compete wasn't easy. To be eligible, golfers had to have a record of ability, tournament victories, and a $300 entry fee.

The weeding-out process began almost immediately with regional tryouts in Riverside, California; Quincy, Illinois; and Winston-Salem, North Carolina. Each of these tournaments consisted of four rounds, and about four of every five starters—282 golfers—were eliminated.

The survivors—seventy-five of us—came to the PGA Na-

tional Golf Club in Palm Beach Gardens, Florida. There, instead of the four rounds that had previously constituted the tournament, it had gone to six rounds. The extra two rounds had been added to make it tougher; if a player got lucky on one round, it wouldn't cancel out poor golf on the other rounds.

The way it turned out, fourteen players failed for every one who made the grade that year. Those are pretty stiff odds. The cutoff was 444 strokes—an average of 74 per round—and not only did those who failed have to wait a year for another chance, but in each new year the odds are again stacked against all but a relative handful.

Besides the pretty lopsided ratio of qualifiers to also-rans, my fellow competitors included many of the players who went on to become some of the top names in the sport: among others, Tom Watson, Lanny Wadkins, Bruce Fleisher, David Graham, Leonard Thompson, and John Mahaffey Jr.

Even the weather conspired to make it a tough test. We played the first round in a day-long rain. We had sun the next two days, then a hot humid Thursday, and finally two pretty decent golf days. After I got my card as a golfing pro, I spent nine years on the Tour, the big leagues of professional golf. It was a postgraduate course in the most challenging of all sports, and in the process I tested my game against the world's most difficult courses.

I learned a lot, and I am going to share that experience with you. But probably no lesson was more important than the one I learned in the tournament in which I turned pro. Like most former college golfers, I had a feeling that the game would somehow change when I went into the play-for-money ranks— that it would become my task now to beat a whole field of super-golfers.

It is true, of course, that at the pro level the caliber of golf is world-class. But what I learned in the transition was that amateur or pro, the game of golf never changes. It isn't the other players who are your true opponents even in "sudden death" overtime. Your real opponent is the golf course itself. Your

challenge is to tackle the course and score the best that you can; all the other golfers in the same event have the same challenge.

That was true in the pro qualifying tournament. For all the famous names in that event, I was not aware—and don't think any of the others were either—of competing against other golfers. The test for all of us was to compete against par; to score well on a very demanding golf course. As it turned out, I put together some of the best golf of my life, rounds of 70, 71, 72, 72, 71, and a final round 69 to become the top qualifier by three strokes.

But while they were six fabulous rounds, a second part of my education, in the years that followed, was to learn that those days of tearing up a golf course don't happen consistently—at least for most of us. As a pro, I scored well enough to make a fair living, but I never achieved my great ambition: To win the National Open.

Yet even though I didn't reach that championship status, my career as a tournament pro was a productive one, because it not only gave me the opportunity to play the game I love, and to play it on an almost full-time basis, but it put me in close contact with all the great and near-great golfers of the modern era.

Playing competitive golf regularly and in the company of top-flight pros probably did more to solidify my game than all the practice rounds I've ever played. I found—and you will too—when you play with golfers whose game is as good as or better than yours, your own game gets better.

One player probably influenced me more than any other. When anybody talks about great golfers—in the days when I broke into the professional ranks, as well as before and since— the name that always stands out is Jack Nicklaus. Even after he passed his competitive prime, he was always the big drawing card, the player to reckon with for top money.

What qualities have made Nicklaus such a great golfer? A sportswriter asked me that question some years ago. At the time I answered in the best way I could, by telling him what I thought would happen if Jack and I were going head-and-head in a major tournament.

I had the ability to shoot sub-par golf. On the practice tee, we would probably look pretty much alike, and there would probably be little difference in our emotional ability or desire to win. But there would be differences between us.

The first major difference would be in the swing. I have a good golf swing, but Nicklaus' is better and, in a match, the better swing will show. That would give him an edge. Moreover, when you get out on the course and the wind starts blowing, a great many other factors come into playing golf.

In fact, there are many things that are a lot easier to do if you're Jack Nicklaus and have a record of more than twenty-five years of success. Besides a lot of experience, he has a big confidence edge. This would show up in almost any match.

Where the difference between us would really have been apparent, however, was in my dream match—Nicklaus and I in a situation in which we were tied in the National Open with four holes left to play. In that setting, he would have had a big advantage.

I would have one thing going for me. Having played sixty-eight holes well enough to be tied for the lead, I could only have been ''hot''; my drives in the fairway, approaches crisp, and my putter dropping the ball into the cup. At that point, I would have great confidence in myself and my game; and a golfer on a streak is hard to beat.

But for everything in my favor, Jack would still have an ''extra'' I didn't have: I have never won the National Open. I'd have to do battle with myself, fighting to keep my confidence and doing everything I could to avoid the ''yippies.''

By contrast, Nicklaus—although not quite as if playing golf with his wife on a Wednesday afternoon—would be a lot more comfortable. He's been under pressure before, and often.

That matchup never occurred, of course. And even at the time I answered that sportswriter I had a feeling my answer wasn't complete. It wasn't enough to recognize that Nicklaus is one of the great golfers of all time, and that there were a lot of reasons for his reputation. I knew them firsthand.

As one of those competing in the same tournaments, I had

many times had the chance to admire firsthand his grooved swing, his all-around game, his instinct for golf, and his winner's temperament. However, many golfers can be said to have those qualities.

Obviously there were more, but it wasn't until I left the tour and became essentially a weekend golfer, playing with the high handicappers, that I finally found the answer.

As I reviewed the list of tournaments over the years, what had really impressed me was not just the mechanics of Nicklaus' game, proficient as he is. The ingredient that really made him a standout was his talent for avoiding errors.

More than anything else, the real mark of his championship caliber was his ability, game after game, year after year, to make fewer mistakes than the rest of us. He didn't always win every tournament he entered, but I never remember seeing Nicklaus beat himself.

What Jack Nicklaus has done with remarkable consistency over the years is to play ''smart golf.'' He has learned a lesson that can be summarized quite simply: When you stop throwing away strokes needlessly, you start to play winning golf. You improve your game most effectively when you search out and eliminate your errors. It is the quickest route I know to success on the golf course.

I have borrowed from that experience. Using that concept, I have been able to teach golfers how to break 100 for the first time in their lives, and have helped 90-shooters take up to 10 strokes off their game. I've also shown low-handicap players how to get down to par golf simply by playing smart golf. I won't guarantee that you'll become another Jack Nicklaus on the golf course, but in this book I will show you how to play better golf by thinking smart golf the way he does.

Probably the best way to start thinking like a professional golfer is to understand what it is like to be a tournament player. Every player on the pro tour is a good golfer; otherwise he wouldn't be there. And all the top golfers play pretty much the same game, except for Tom Watson.

For many years what made Watson different was his driving, and that was the chief reason why many professionals doubted that he would ever win the National Open or the PGA championship. In his earlier days, Watson just didn't drive as well as some other top golfers. He simply wasn't as accurate.

Thus, other pros felt that Watson could win plenty of tournaments but not the Open, because more than any other, it puts a premium on accuracy off the tee. On demanding courses like Pebble Beach, therefore, most of us tended to write off Tom Watson in favor of better drivers like Calvin Peete, Hubert Green, Hale Irwin, and others who usually do well in the tournament.

In his earlier days as a pro, Watson was up among the top players even without a strong game off the tee and for one good reason—he had the ability to score well even when he played poorly. In fact, he could play horribly—miss many of the fairways with his tee shots—and still come in with a 71 when most other pros having the same kind of problems would have posted a 76 or 77.

Watson wasn't content to be a scrambler, however, and he kept working on his weaknesses until 1982, when he began to put his whole game together. His drives became ever straighter, and combined with his scrambling talents, pushed him into the forefront of golf. No longer was it possible to ignore him when predicting the likely winner of the PGA or National Open.

His better driving added another dimension to Watson's already great game. There is a good reason why driving plays such an important role in tournament play. It markedly improves your percentages. There are fourteen holes on a golf course where you hit a drive off the tee. Every time your drive stops in the fairway the odds on hitting a good second shot improve; every time your drive goes into the rough, your success ratio goes down.

There is another reason for its importance on the tournament circuit. On the tour, almost everybody hits within a twenty-yard range. But when someone is playing well, he develops

confidence in his abilities and begins to hit harder and longer—as well as straighter—drives. It pays off.

Even more important in finally breaking Watson's personal jinx and enabling him to win the 1982 Open, was his ability to play well and recover from his errors. You may recall his dramatic sixteen-foot chip shot on the seventy-first hole at Pebble Beach that gave him the title.

In many ways Watson got to that pressure shot in typical fashion. Late in the first round he was three over par, but he then put together three straight birdies. On the second day his driving was terrible, but on two occasions he saved himself with putts of more than twenty feet. "I shot a 77, but scored a 72," he said—a comment he could have made many times in his career.

The next day Watson got hot and shot a four-under par 68 to tie Bill Rogers going into the final round. Jack Nicklaus was three strokes behind of both of them with eighteen holes to go. Then, as he had done so often in the past, Nicklaus went on a streak and produced a great round of 69 to come into the clubhouse at four-under par for the seventy-two holes and what appeared to be a sure victory.

Meanwhile, Watson was still out on the course, and he too was playing well. He had been driving extremely well all day long and while making some mistakes was compensating for them on the greens. With a twenty-five footer on the tenth hole and a thirty-five footer on the fourteenth, he proved once more that he may be the finest long putter in the game.

By the time Watson got to the seventeenth hole he was clearly in the money, but off the tee his 2-iron shot bounced into an uphill slope to the left of the green. It presented a well-nigh impossible shot, because the green on that hole was so fast that there wasn't room for the ball to stop.

Watson's caddy gave him encouragement. "Get it close," he said.

"I'm not going to get it close," replied Watson, "I'm going to make it."

He opened up the face of his wedge and laid the ball softly

onto the putting surface. Even so, it ran and might have kept on going had it not struck the flag and dropped into the cup. That shot became a golf legend and, in the opinion of most of the sportswriters who covered the tournament, was the shot that gave Watson his first National Open.

Probably no other golfer could have made that shot. Even Jack Nicklaus labeled it a one-in-a-thousand shot, but it was no fluke. Watson had practiced for years hitting shots out of high grass, and this was the day it paid off.

Although that chip shot got most of the attention in the tournament, I disagree with the golf writers. It is my opinion that Watson won the tournament on the sixteenth and not the seventeenth hole. The sixteenth hole at Pebble Beach is a real terror, and almost impossible to understand how difficult to play for a golfer who has never played it under tournament conditions. Earlier, when the National Open was first played at Pebble Beach, the sixteenth wasn't merely difficult; without an accurate drive it was impossible.

In most tournaments, you can often recover from a poor drive on the shorter holes by rolling the ball up onto the green with your second shot. The tournament committee took away that option on the sixteenth green by letting the rough grow right up to the edge of the green to prevent a run-up shot. The alternative route—a pitch to the green—was also effectively ruled out because the greens were like concrete and a ball wouldn't stop running. The only remaining chance for a birdie or even a par was to hit a shot just at the edge of the rough and hope it took one bounce and slowed down enough to stay on the green. This made it a matter of luck rather than a test of golfing skill.

This time the tournament committee didn't present that impossible challenge, but did toughen up the sixteenth hole with a new trap to the right of the fairway, just about fifteen yards away from where a perfect drive would have to land.

It is my belief that Tom Watson was playing to win and trying for that perfect drive. He played it close, deliberately

"hugging" the right edge of the fairway with his drive so he could have the best angle for his second shot to the green.

However, he made an error in his swing, which—while probably only a small error—was enough to carry his ball more right than he wanted, and it landed in the trap. At this point Watson faced the first of a series of decisions upon which he would win or lose the tournament.

This was a tough bunker. It had a high lip; above the lip was about eighteen inches of high, thick grass. There were still about 160 yards to go to the green; and between the trap and the green was a forty-yard-wide drainage ditch.

It is highly unlikely that even a perfect shot would have overcome the combination of those difficulties. So the first decision Watson made was not to try the impossible.

Instead, he wisely chipped the ball out sideways from the trap and onto the fairway to the spot where a perfect drive would have landed. Even at this point, Watson had a very difficult shot.

The pin was placed in the left front of the green, leaving only a small target for his approach shot. Moreover, the green was lightning fast, and angled straight down toward the Beach House. A poor shot would have meant a double-bogey or worse, enough to put Watson out of the running for the championship.

Watson hit just the right kind of shot to the green, so that even though it rolled, it just barely rolled off the putting surface onto the fringe. He was able to use his putter to put the ball within three feet of the cup, and holed his second putt.

It was a bogey hole that might not have looked good to somebody who saw only the scorecard. But in my opinion, Watson would not have won the Open if he hadn't had the wisdom to hit a safety shot out of the sand trap and follow up with a fine approach shot. We'll talk more about that later.

If you put Tom Watson in a class by himself, you'll find that most other golfers on the tour play pretty much the same game. But even with those similarities, every one is an individual, with his own abilities and limitations and his own approach to

the game. This means that there is no ironclad way to play golf; no single approach that works well for everybody, professional or amateur; no one answer that is universal for all players.

You don't have to be big to play good golf. Bobby Cole weighs in at about 140 pounds, yet I have never played with anyone who hits the ball farther.

Just about everybody overrates distance as the mark of a good golfer. In the pro ranks, if you have a good golf swing, you seem to hit the ball in the range of 240 to 270 yards. Any more yardage just doesn't make much difference. As a matter of fact, it can be a liability.

This is also true for the amateur. Sure, there is great satisfaction in being a long hitter. But a smart pro will trade position for distance every time. As I'll prove to you, it's a lot better to give up those extra yards if it means keeping the ball in the fairway.

You'd think that a tall player would have an advantage. The arc of his swing is longer and he ought to be able to generate a great deal more clubhead speed. But it doesn't seem to work out that way. About the only good hitters I've ever seen who are over six-feet tall are Tom Weiskopf, Andy Bean, and John Miller. George Archer and Howard Twiddy are very tall, and they can belt the ball a mile, but they have trouble being consistent.

In my experience, most of the good golfers on the pro tour are about five-foot ten. Many—such as Bill Rogers, Tom Watson and Tom Kite—also have about the same build; one may be thinner and one a little stronger, but all measure under six feet. That includes one player who comes close to my ideal: Lanny Wadkins, who always gives the impression of being in control of his swing and his game.

I get the feeling that you could take away Wadkins' clubs for two years and he would return and pick up right where he left off.

Regardless of which player you choose, there is one characteristic of today's pro. He is a better player using better equipment than his counterpart of ten or more years ago. This

doesn't mean that today's best golfer is superior to those of the past; the winning scores really haven't come down that much. Instead, competition has gotten tighter. If you read down the scores in a current tournament, you'll probably find more players bunched in the lower-scoring range. In fact, I think the day is rapidly approaching when the cutoff for the PGA Tour will go below 140; sub-par scores will be needed in the first two rounds in order to qualify for the final two rounds.

The major changes in golf are attributable to television. TV brought the big money to golf, and that, in turn, has encouraged more good amateurs to try the play-for-pay approach. Television has also done more, for while tournaments have always drawn their galleries of enthusiasts to watch the great players in action, you no longer have to visit the site in person.

Today, anybody can watch the best in golf from around the world. These days, when I'm not on the tour, I'm keeping up to date by watching on the tube. This isn't just good TV entertainment; it is a great way to go to golf school.

When I was playing in person against some of the stars I now watch on television, I picked up some valuable pointers. But whereas the touring pro is so involved in his own game that he has only a limited opportunity to learn, television gives everyone both a close-up view of his special favorites and the chance to see firsthand how a variety of players react to similar golfing problems.

For example, every golfer gets into trouble at some time during a round. This is especially true of the high handicap player. For getting out of trouble, you couldn't get a better teacher than Tom Watson. He is an expert at it, possibly because he seems to get into more golfing problems than most.

If you pay attention to Watson's play in almost any tournament, you'll see him emerging from at least one tough dilemma, and often more. His key to success—as mentioned earlier—is never seeming to try to do the impossible.

Watson recognizes that the most important thing for him is to get out of trouble and to have a chance at recovery, as witnessed by his safety shot out of the sixteenth-hole bunker in the

1982 Open. He uses a winning blend of all-out effort modified by caution. In fact, it is almost a trademark of Watson's game that he recognizes that there are times when you have to bite the bullet and lose a shot now in the hope of making it up later.

By itself, that one lesson can save any golfer from one to five shots in a single round, and save even more for the duffer. Trade off a single shot in favor of safety rather than gamble on the difficult or near-impossible shot.

There are other lessons you can learn by watching golf on TV. Much of the action is in and around the greens, and you can pick up a number of pointers on the short game and on styles of putting. In particular it pays to watch the care with which the top golfers size up their putts, often from different angles.

Note as well the putts that they miss. The top players don't sink them all, but do know how to consistently putt the ball close to the hole—another mark of a good player.

Nonetheless, I should voice a word of caution. While TV can be a learning experience, it has limitations. For one thing, it is very easy to get the wrong impression of professional golf from television. What you view are the final holes of a tournament. Only the best players are featured—the ones who are all hitting the ball straight; only rarely will you see a top contender spraying shots all over the place.

As a result, you don't see much bad golf. Nor do you see the great shots that enabled the top finishers to be in contention. Most of what appears on your screen is putting. True, that's ultimately where most close tournaments are won or lost. But a lot more than putting goes into a round of golf.

One of the things you have probably never seen on television is a professional losing his golf ball. As a matter of fact, most high handicappers think it doesn't happen to a pro. But believe me, it happens a lot more often than you think. And it has happened to me.

I lost a ball at the 1977 U.S. Open at Pebble Beach even though the marshals knew exactly where it went. It was on the par-three fifth hole. It's a short hole, but tricky, with a small,

L-shaped green that slopes to the right toward the ocean. The long part of the L runs across the fairway and at the base of the L is a trap.

When the pin is on the left, you try to scoot the ball by that bunker. When it is on the right, you have to carry the hazard. This day the pin was on the right, which meant you had to go over the trap to reach the green. I hit a shot that I thought would come down right at the hole. Instead it plunked into the trap.

Sometimes, right before a National Open, they put new sand in the bunkers, and this was one of those times. New sand hasn't had a chance to absorb moisture, and so is very soft. With five inches of new sand and the pitch of that bunker, the ball disappeared without a trace.

Although each player in a tournament is responsible for his own ball, the marshals are encouraged to help, in the interest of speeding up the game, and they did. So did the others in my threesome. But all in vain. While the marshals pointed to the exact spot where the ball fell, we never found it. The lost ball cost me a penalty and I had to hit my shot again, a tough break when you're on the money circuit. So, while you may not find it much consolation, the next time your ball seems to become "invisible," you'll know that it happens to all of us at one time or another.

Another thing that happens—even if only rarely—is for a pro to miss the ball completely in his swing, just like the most rank amateur. Sometimes it is carelessness that causes this, but it is also possible to "whiff" a legitimate shot, particularly in heavy rough.

In matted rough, you don't have any contact with the ball; the grass is in the way. Occasionally, however, the ball sets up in the rough and you can go right under it with a sand wedge.

It is also possible to whiff a short putt. Gary Groh won the 1975 Hawaiian Open despite missing a putt on the second hole. Here's what happened. Having missed an approach putt, he became irritated with himself, reached across the hole to back-hand the ball into the hole, and missed it completely.

Fortunately, Groh went on to win the event by two strokes,

so that the error didn't cost him the victory. But it did give him a chance to make a wise observation. Asked what his feelings would have been had he lost the tournament by that missed putt, he replied by saying, "I would still have felt OK. I hadn't won a tournament all year," he explained, and "If I only lost by one stroke, it meant I had to have been playing pretty good."

Despite this, I still don't advise blowing those short putts. It's hard enough making the long ones without giving away the easy ones.

Pro and amateur golfers share more than just lost golf balls, whiffs, and mistakes. They also share temperament. The average golfer may think that he's the only one who gets nervous when he tees up on the first hole, but I can assure you that everybody, at some time, gets the jitters.

In my career, I had some great golf thrills at Oakmont—for many years the golfing home of Arnold Palmer, another of the game's great players. I finished fourth in the national amateur there in 1969, which earned me an invitation to the Masters. But Oakmont is also the place where I got a king-sized case of the butterflies.

Although every player in a tournament is keyed up, especially before a big round, you usually lose all your nervousness as soon as you hit the first shot. Until then, however, you think you'll never get over it. My big dose of jitters came in the 1978 PGA championship. That was the year John Mahaffey won in a playoff with Jerry Pate and Tom Watson.

I shot a 69 and a 72 on the first two days, which were excellent scores, and was in a tie for third place. But Pittsburgh—where Oakmont is located—is in the western part of the eastern time zone of the United States, and stays light until very late in August. On that night, it wasn't all that easy to sleep, and I did a lot of tossing and turning.

Normally, if I had been back in the pack, I would probably have been out on the course before noon. But because I was among the leaders in the tournament, my schedule was changed. The players with the lowest scores tee off to accom-

modate the big crowds, and our tee-off time was 3:30 P.M. It meant that I had a lot of extra time in which to do nothing except look forward to the round. That added to the pressure.

Then there was the crowd. The spectators were so jammed together that it took two security guards to escort us the thirty yards from the putting green to the first tee—after which they had to fight their way back to get our caddies and clubs.

I was hitting third—the honor was determined by the way the scores came in the day before—and Ben Crenshaw led off. Ben got a good drive. Now I was really afraid that everyone else would hit good solid drives, and I would embarrass myself by hitting a poor one.

Nevertheless, Tom Weiskopf hitting second promptly duck-hooked the ball. That proved to be the magic cure. When I saw how badly Tom had hit his shot, I immediately became less nervous; I was confident I wouldn't hit one quite that bad and I didn't. The thought enabled me to settle down and play good golf.

Curiously enough, that first bad drive helped Tom Weiskopf. There was something about his experience in that tournament that every golfer must learn on his way to smart golf. Tom didn't let it get him down. Perhaps he felt he wouldn't hit another ball that poorly again in the round. And he didn't. I think he shot a 68 that day—six birdies and an eagle.

Too many people have a mental barrier; you may have experienced it yourself. You hit a bad first drive and it throws off your whole game because you brood about it.

Or you get off the tee in pretty good shape and then things go wrong. This happens frequently to the weekend golfer. He starts out on the first hole and makes a 7 or, depending on his game, some score higher than he had hoped. And he lets that ruin his whole day.

There's an obvious lesson: Sure it's a lot better to start out well, but it doesn't make sense to let down because of a poor first drive. Nor does it make sense to give up because of a bad first hole; there are still seventeen more to go, plenty of time to make up lost strokes.

What you can do under such circumstances is to put that first hole out of your mind for the time being. Then, when you have finished playing for the day, you can analyze where you went wrong—what it was that produced the bad score. In my experience, it is usually traceable to one shot in which you didn't have the percentages in your favor; then you gambled—and lost—in an effort to make it up.

Good golfing habits come from disciplining yourself so that you learn to put the bad shots and the bad holes behind you, then move on to the next challenge.

Sometimes you have to do that on the early holes. But it can also happen later on. In fact, a second psychological barrier sometimes comes when you're playing great golf and there is a real possibility that you will set a new low score. Thus, for example, you may be on the eighteenth tee, having only to shoot a 6 to break 90. All too often, you wind up with a 7 trying to make that 6.

The two problems—dwelling on a prior shot that failed or looking too far ahead—stem from the same cause. What has happened is that you have lost sight of your objective. You have stopped concentrating on the shot you are attempting right now. And that's a mistake.

You have to drum it into your golf philosophy that nothing can influence what has already happened. Nor can you allow yourself to daydream about the future. You can't reach the tenth hole and start congratulating yourself on what a fine round you've got going; you still have nine holes to play.

There are four simple rules that make up one of the great lessons of golf:

1. You can do nothing about the shot you've already played.
2. You can't shoot the next shot until you've completed the one you are now attempting.
3. The most important shot in your current round is the one you're about to make.

4. You must play the golf course, not your golfing companions.

One of the toughest challenges in golf is to resist the urge to outdo the other guy. I've already mentioned my imaginary shootout with Jack Nicklaus. If he and I were playing all even on the seventy-second hole of a major tournament, my biggest problem wouldn't be Nicklaus, it would be me. It would be important not to let me beat myself. Let me explain.

You beat yourself when you start playing the other fellow rather than the golf course. This isn't always an easy lesson to learn. If on the final hole Nicklaus had the honor and hit a perfect shot off the tee, for example, it would be easy for me to lose control. My natural instinct would be to try to match that shot and put an extra squeeze on the club. That usually makes a tough shot tougher.

When that kind of critical moment occurs, it is essential to maintain confidence in your own game. As they say in football, stick to your game plan. Play the golf course, not your opponent. You don't know what he is going to do with the remainder of his game; and it really doesn't make any difference—unless you let it.

If you play the course well, you still have a chance to overcome your opponent's great shot and win. To do that, you've got to concentrate on your game, not his. And that takes confidence.

I remember playing with Watson and John Schlee in the last round of the PGA championship in Washington, D.C. We were in the third-from-last group, which meant that we had a chance at the championship.

Schlee had the best chance. But he was very nervous and, as we waited to tee off on the seventeenth, he remarked that he wished he could par the last two holes. This was understandable because those were very difficult holes. Par would probably bring him in fifth and pay $10,000 or more.

Watson had a different idea. "Instead of trying for par, why don't you birdie the next two holes and win the tournament,"

17

he said. That's how winners think, and that's how you must train yourself to think if you want to play winning golf.

Schlee tried to follow Watson's advice. He played well on 17 and 18, but he couldn't pick up the birdies. As I remember, he wound up fourth or fifth.

The rules for good golf apply to amateur and professional alike. But there are differences in the way the game is played. Let me tell you about a few; it will help you understand the difference between the game you see on TV and the one you play on your home course.

Surprisingly enough, the pro has some advantages over the average golfer. For example, although he plays on courses that are deliberately toughened up for a tournament, they are fair. For one thing, the traps are consistent. One bunker won't be soft and the next one hard, so that the player will never know which is which until he has been in all of them. Normally, if you are in a trap on the first hole in a pro tournament, you can anticipate that all of them are going to be similar.

The weekend player doesn't have the same assurance. If he plays Wednesday the traps may play soft, but on Friday so hard they bounce his ball back out—an inequality of playing on public links or courses that are not set up.

In fact, consistency is all a pro asks of a golf course. He doesn't want the greenskeepers to water the first half of the first green and the second half of the second green. Yet this was one trick that was used years ago at Tam O'Shanter in Chicago.

My brother and I both caddied at Tam. It was George S. May's course and he brought big money to golf. On the back nine at Tam were four holes—the tenth, twelfth, thirteenth, and fourteenth—before you came across the road to finish at the clubhouse. The twelfth, thirteenth, and fourteenth were long par-4s where you had to hit 4- and 5-irons to reach the green.

The greens were sizeable, maybe 2,500 square feet. They appeared to be fair targets, but if the first 1,200 square feet were watered and the second half left untouched, it created a "secret" hazard.

The greens were slightly elevated. This meant that you had to shoot to the green itself. If you hit the front, where the ground was softened, the ball would stop dead; if you hit the middle of the green the ball would keep right on rolling off the putting surface.

Either way, it made it almost impossible to play well on those holes because you were getting results that were not indicative of the shot you were hitting. It not only threw you off, but disturbed your golfing judgment on the final holes.

In bygone years the PGA didn't run the tournaments; instead, it was often customary to let the home club do this. And they would never set the course up the way they would have liked to play it themselves. Quite the contrary. They didn't want the pros to ''chew up'' their course with a lot of sub-par rounds; it would tell the golfing world that they had an ''easy'' course.

So they tried to make it impossible to score well. They used such tricks as rolling half the greens with 500-pound rollers and watering the other half. When part of the green is hard and part is soft, it becomes impossible to play with skill. Another trick was to shave the greens down by three-sixteenths of an inch, perhaps to one-eighth inch. This makes them like concrete, and is the surest way to make any golf course tough.

If you play public courses or ones that are not regularly maintained and watered, you are likely to encounter these treacherous playing conditions—dried out greens, rock-hard fairways, ill-kept and variable sand traps.

Take advantage of the situation. The rest of your foursome is going to be playing under the same conditions; if you are alert to these special problems, you should be able to pick up a shot or two on those who are simply playing the course blindly.

By comparison with the past, the people in charge of a PGA tournament are always seeking fairness. Their sole objective is to make the course play in such a way that the best player wins. They do it by consistency. They never mow the rough after the competition begins. The fairways are always cut the afternoon

19

before the first day of a tournament and again after the first, second, and third rounds.

Even so, the PGA can't make matters completely fair. Those who play in the morning come out while there is dew on the ground and the wetness makes it more difficult to control the ball. Those who draw afternoon play find the grass has grown a little longer, which also causes the ball to jump. It's like playing in rain; the good news is that the ball is going to stop when it hits the ground; the bad news is that you don't know *where* it's going to hit.

The high-handicap player doesn't pay attention to these details. He'll play the same at seven in the morning as he does at six at night. It compounds his problem. Not only is he not sure just how he will hit a ball, but he hasn't learned what the ball will do if he does everything right. He hasn't learned to "read" a shot. Reading a shot is very important; failing to do so is like reading a book and missing half the words.

Weather, and its impact on playing conditions, is very significant. In the 1973 National Open, Johnny Miller shot a 63 at Oakmont. It happened only because it had rained the night before the fourth round. This softened the greens and the shots held.

Miller played perfect golf that day. His approach game was on target and his play on the greens superb. As the pros say, he created the opportunities with his irons and took advantage of them with his putter.

I played in that National Open, but not very well. I made the cut but finished way down on the list. When I played that same course five years later in the PGA, I played much better.

As a matter of fact, I might have had a chance to finish in the first five in the 1978 PGA championship except that on the afternoon of the third round, I three-putted four greens in the second nine and shot a 74. That's not a bad score, but it would have been a great round without those extra putts. Those are the "ifs" that haunt the pro just as much as they haunt a weekend golfer.

I am often asked about the difference between playing tour-

nament golf and playing in a regular foursome. There is probably more pressure in tournament competition because you are not playing only a single round, but four, and it is the four-round total that you get paid for.

But in terms of how you play, I don't think there is that much difference. In a tournament you still have to attack the course. You have to play aggressive golf.

By aggressive golf I don't mean riverboat-gambler golf. On the contrary, aggressive golf in championship play is really fundamental golf in two ways:

1. It means hitting the ball in the fairway.
2. It involves trying to get your next shot on the green.

As a matter of fact, you don't even have to get the shot close to the hole, although it's a plus if you do.

If you'll think about it, this is also good advice for the high-handicap golfer, and in my opinion, good golf requires good thinking. There are two parts of golf—physical and mental. Almost any golfer can improve his physical approach to the game. The only limitations are his physical talents. Not everybody is going to be physically capable of driving a golf ball 300 yards or of powering a ball out of super-heavy rough.

But there is another side of golf that has almost no limits— the ability to "think" good golf. Too many golfers focus on their physical game and ignore the mental side. Yet it is in the thinking phase of the game that a golfer can achieve the most improvement.

It always amazes me that a duffer will spend money on golf lessons and never seem to learn anything about the game. He or she simply continues to repeat the same errors, which are usually errors caused by faulty thinking.

Even among the pros there are golfers who play pretty much by rote. They may be quite expert mechanically, but they lack the extra edge that comes to the player who "thinks" his way around the course.

21

The classic case of a golfer who had all the tools for the game plus an ability to apply his intellect is Ben Hogan.

On the tenth and twelfth holes at Oakmont, Hogan deliberately hit the ball long, taking a chance of going over the green. Ordinarily this is one of the worst shots in golf, but Hogan had spent time studying the slope of the two greens and noticed something that almost everybody else had noticed but failed to realize: The greens sloped away from the fairway, as opposed to most greens, which slope toward the drainage area in front of the green.

Hogan's keen observation of the terrain enabled him to reverse the normal strategy. By shooting long and coming back toward the hole, he left himself a favorable uphill chip shot.

When you play these three holes you can appreciate Hogan's unorthodox wisdom. The greens are pitched downward, possibly as much as 14 degrees; that plus hard greens meant that it was fatal to leave your second shot short of the green.

Even if you had only a short chip shot, it was an automatic bogey-5 to land in front of the green. The combination of slope and hardness would carry your ball fifteen feet past the hole. Hogan's uphill chip was a lot easier to control.

You probably aren't going to encounter many of these "reverse" greens, but when you do, remember the Hogan trick. Even more important, remember that it was this kind of thinking that made Hogan a great golfer; good golfers are always on the lookout for that extra edge that helps bring their scores down.

I'd like to emphasize that Hogan's tactic of shooting long on those holes was a rarity. In almost every case the reverse is true. As a matter of fact, here is a tip that can help you save strokes consistently:

If in doubt, aim for the part of the fairway in front of the green. In most cases this is a high-percentage shot. If you make the green, fine. But even if you don't, you'll have the whole green to shoot for on your chip shot.

Add another factor. The odds are with you even if you make a mistake on your approach. If you're short, the front of the

green is usually cut like the fairway, and you'll probably have a good lie.

Avoid shooting long. If you gamble and go over the green, you're in thick trouble. The area in back of the green is usually unkempt and rough and, if that isn't bad enough, the greens usually slope forward and the shot back to the cup must come downhill.

It's a simple matter of playing the favorable odds. Always allow for errors. You are going to make them; everybody does; but try to make those mistakes where you have the greatest room for error. If you can't play perfect golf—and nobody can—making every effort to keep the odds in your favor takes some of the gamble out of golf.

In making the personal transition from tournament play to weekend golf, I re-learned this simple fact, and it has helped me gain a greater understanding of the needs of the average player.

I have been impressed with the strong desire of most golfers I meet to improve their game; yet all too often they are simply repeating, over and over again, the same mistakes.

One is in their viewpoint. It is easy to imagine how your golf score would shrink to par and below if only you could learn to drive like Nicklaus, recover like Watson, swing like Wadkins, and putt like the current "hot" golfer on the tour.

That's the typical approach of many golf books, but in my opinion it is based on only a single view of golf: That it is a game in which you try to take the fewest strokes to get the ball into the cup eighteen times in a round.

As a result, many people believe that the answer to improving their game is to hit the ball farther, sharpen their iron game, increase their accuracy in approaching the green, and learn how to sink their putts.

This is, of course, one way to look at golf. But it is an oversimplified view, and it doesn't work for most golfers. Why? Because it is based on the theory that if you do everything right, you'll shoot a perfect game.

But never in the history of golf has anyone shot a perfect game, nor will any golfer ever play a totally errorless round. It is simply not possible. Jack Nicklaus, Arnold Palmer, Bobby Jones, Ben Hogan—and all of the greats of golf—never shot a flawless round, however close they may sometimes have come.

To put it another way, even the best golfers make mistakes. They are great golfers simply because they make fewer mistakes than the rest of us. That is the basis for my approach to golf. You learn to play better golf by learning how to avoid mistakes. And the best way to do this is to concentrate on mental errors.

I see the 100 shooter all the time. In most cases the reasons he consistently fails to break 100 are mental errors. He has the physical ability to shoot respectable golf, but fails—and keeps on failing—to get his score down into the 90s or lower because of poor thinking on the course.

At the club where I now play most of the time, we don't really have many great players. Our membership is pretty average. Typically, my beginner will take his first shot of the day and drive it into the right rough, and almost without exception will follow this with another poor shot.

Rather than getting the next shot back onto the fairway, he will instead take another swing and perhaps hit the ball 100 yards, but still have it in the right rough. Thus, while he has gotten closer to the green, he hasn't bettered his odds for the next shot.

Nor does this situation occur only with a drive into the rough. How many times have you seen a player up against a tree? Instead of hitting his ball straight sideways and back onto the fairway, he'll try to go forward, thinking he can pull off a great golf shot when in fact he can't.

Or take the player who tees off on a 400-yard hole and hits the ball his maximum distance of 200 yards. He still has 200 yards to go to reach the green. Even with his best second shot he can't get the ball to the green. Yet he will try.

He'll even try that same shot when he's in the rough—a doubly impossible situation.

And if our friend avoids that mistake, he is likely to make another. Rather than using a club with less distance but which he can control, he will invariably reach for the club with which he hits (or thinks he hits) the farthest.

Had he only used the proper club, he could have put the ball out in front of the green, where he would have a good third shot. But this doesn't seem to occur to him. Instead he will try to hit a 3-wood and aim for the green. And because he usually doesn't have command of that club, the result is typically a bad shot. On the other hand, had he hit a good 4-iron, he would have been short of the green but in a position to pitch to the middle of it, with a chance for a one-putt hole. Fortunately, such mental errors are the easiest to eliminate if you learn "smart" golf.

Smart golf is realistic golf.

We all recognize that luck plays a role in every sport, including golf. There are days when a long, tough putt drops in, an approach shot has "eyes," and the long wood and iron shots soar extra yards. But many amateurs never seem to learn that luck also evens out, good and bad, and that in the long run it isn't luck, but ability that counts.

The physical part of my game improves when I play against top-flight golfers. But the rest of my game has improved since I have been working with high-handicap players.

Since I left the tournament trail, I have found that I still have the ability on any given day to play as well as I ever did. As a matter of fact, in October 1984 I shot a 62 at Ridgemoor Country Club in Chicago. It tied the course record set by Ben Hogan in 1942 when he won the Victory Cup, the wartime version of the U.S. Open. But I am not as consistent as I was in my days on the Tour. It is unlikely that I could count on putting together four straight days of par and sub-par golf, the kind of golf you need to win on the road.

One reason for the loss of consistency is that I don't practice as much as I did on the Tour, which comes down to not hitting

as many golf balls as I did when I was making my living playing golf.

The reality of competitive golf is that nobody who plays, as I now do, on an occasional basis, can score well day-in and day-out. Only constant play under competitive conditions will develop the touch in and around the greens that you must have to win a professional tournament.

If I were to go back for the National Open, for example, I would have to undertake a rigorous training session and concentrate on steady play to tighten up my game.

Still, I do know that there is one way in which my game has improved. Now, even more so than when I played the Tour, I play percentage golf. I think better on the course. I always try to hit the shot that is possible.

A lot of times in my tournament days, I would try to hit the impossible shot and wind up making flagrant mistakes like going over the green. I used to do that often; today I don't make that mistake any more. Nor any longer do I find myself aiming the ball above the pin, where I couldn't possibly make it pay out even if I hit the perfect shot and then sank a ten-foot putt.

I still make mistakes, and I sometimes still wind up in the wrong place through poor shooting, but almost never from trying too hard. These days, if I hit the shot I'm trying for, I rarely end up in a mess. My errors are usually not thinking errors. In many ways, I am my own best student.

I've "gone to school" on the errors of the high handicapper. Having spotted the way in which duffers needlessly lose strokes to par, I now make more of a conscious effort to make my errors on the side of the fairway, or of the pin, that favors me.

One simple example. When the pin is in the back right corner of the green, I always attempt to hit to the left rather than to the right of the hole.

I've also developed a habit of reminding myself why Jack Nicklaus was so tough to beat.

When I first joined the pro tour, I had great ambitions, in-

cluding, as I've mentioned, beating Nicklaus. And if beating Nicklaus meant finishing higher in the standings in a given tournament, I did, probably twice a year.

But I never had a real shootout match with Jack; the closest I came was probably in team play.

For many years Joe Porter and I teamed up in the Walt Disney World National Team Championship at Lake Buena Vista, Florida. It is a best-ball tournament; the lower score, between you and your partner on each hole, counts.

The top names in golf compete each year and the going is tough; only sub-par teams can even survive the cut. Joe got married just before the 1974 tournament and I was part of the wedding party. We teamed up for the ceremony and, as it turned out, teamed up just as well on the golf course.

The Disney World tourney suited our long-hitting game. We came in the first day with a 64 and then took the tournament lead with a second round 60. At the end of three days, Joe and I added a 66 and led Nicklaus and his partner, Tom Weiskopf, by four strokes.

We held off their challenge in the final round to wind up two strokes ahead of those two great golfers. Our only problem was that there were other teams also competing, and even though we had a personal victory, it was three strokes too many and good for only fifth place.

As a result of competing with great players like Nicklaus, I've never lost my desire to win. And to set my goals I have had to examine my golf game realistically.

I want you to develop the same realism about your game. To realize that at the moment, you aren't going to hit that 250-yard drive or super-shot to reach the green, or can that forty-foot putt.

This doesn't mean that you're settling for second best. Given time you'll be able to make many of the shots that are now beyond your ability. But for the time being, you are going to have to learn to live within your golf means—and let talent, not wishful thinking, measure your improvement.

If you are tempted—and we all are—to stretch that ability,

just remind yourself of your limitations. One way is to think of Jack Nicklaus. Before you try to pull off that miracle shot, pause for a moment and ask yourself, "Who do you think you are—Jack Nicklaus?" Or, you can tell yourself, "Even Nicklaus probably wouldn't make this shot, but I'm going to try it anyway," and then add: "Is that smart?"

If you're honest with yourself, you'll start playing "within yourself."

As I tell my students. "I can't beat Jack Nicklaus; I don't think you can either."

A brief review.

No two golfers play the same game, nor is there a universal approach to good golf. Each player must develop within his own abilities and limitations. Given this, the most effective way to improve your game is to search out and eliminate your errors. Learn to play "smart" golf.

Take a lesson from Tom Watson. When you're in trouble, think your way out. Give your top priority to minimizing the damage, giving up a shot now rather than compounding your error. Identify what you can and can't do on the golf course. Develop a confidence in the shots you attempt. The more confidence you develop, the greater your chance of success. Then play the golf course, not your opponent.

Learn to "read" your shots—the weather, the condition of the course, the lie of the ball. Develop your golf strength through a sound imagination.

Follow the lead of the professional and establish basic goals:

- Keep the ball in the fairway.
- Get your approach shot on the green.

If you do both, you're on your way to low-scoring golf.

Finally, don't pretend you're Jack Nicklaus. You're not.

Chapter 2

Warming Up
—The Right Way

In just a little while, we are going to play a round of golf. But before we rush out to the first tee, let's take time out to plan our strategy. The scene isn't important. It could be my own home course, Ridge Country Club; Butler, Medinah, Kemper Lakes, or any of the other top courses in the Chicago area; or any of the hundred or so courses around the country where I have played over the years.

Or it could be the course where you play golf.

The basics for almost all golf courses are the same. With the exception of the occasional nine-hole course, there are only a few ways a golf course can be laid out. Normally there are four short par-3 holes, three or four par-5s, and the rest are par-4s. The fairway may be a straightaway, a dogleg right or dogleg left, or a combination of these.

The hazards are the rough, sand, water, trees, and shrubs. With these fundamental tools, the golf architect takes advantage of the terrain, the natural landscaping, his budget, and a lot of imagination to produce the most challenging and efficient layout he can design.

On this particular day we're going to play at Olympia Fields, a fine old golf club about thirty miles southwest of Chicago. It has two 18-hole courses; we are going to play the north course. This course has been the scene of many famous championship

29

tournaments. The PGA was held here in 1925 and 1961, the U.S. Open in 1928, and the Western Open in 1920, 1927, 1933, 1968, and 1971.

As we walk the fairways of Olympia Fields, I want you to imagine that you're on your own home course. It won't be the same, naturally. No two courses are exactly alike. The location of the hazards will be different; so will the length and layout of the course and the wind and weather.

But if you stop and think about it, not only are no two courses alike, but even the one course you may play regularly never plays precisely the same on successive days. There are just too many variables, and that is one of the fascinations of golf—the never-ending list of challenges.

Yet even though courses vary, sometimes a great deal, there are also similarities. Thus, while I'm going to describe a round of golf at Olympia Fields, you should, if you use your knowledge of your own home course, be able to apply the same concepts the next time you play. All you have to do is adjust what I'm describing to fit your special needs.

I will be describing each hole at Olympia Fields, how I want to play it, and why. I'll take you inside my golf thinking to point out the step-by-step process that enables a pro to actively challenge a golf course rather than passively react to it.

If you apply these same general guidelines and tailor them to your own course and your own game, you can start on the road to better golf.

A round of golf doesn't start with the first drive—or at least not a good round.

It begins even before the golfer arrives at the clubhouse. The smart player knows there are some things he can check out in advance. The weather plays a big part in determining how a golf course plays on a given day. A series of rainy days will produce greens that "hold" approach shots better; a dry spell can bake the course and give extra roll on the fairways.

An overcast day will make it tougher to gauge distance. It also means the air is "heavy" and a ball won't carry as well.

By contrast, if you are playing in high-altitude country the air is lighter and the ball really carries.

Just a month after I turned pro I played in the Mexican Open, and can still recall the extra distance I got. I normally hit a 6-iron about 170 yards; in the Mexican Open the ball was traveling 195 yards. Those same percentages applied throughout my whole set of clubs; my drives were booming out close to 290 yards. Yet nothing had changed about my game; the only thing different was the higher altitude.

I also remember the trees. They seemed to me the biggest and widest trees I had ever seen. They were so thick that if your shot went off line you almost hoped it would hit a tree, because it seemed easier to play from the rough than to try to find some way back onto the fairway through that solid wall of trunks and branches.

Trees always add a hazard to any golf course, and in the fall they add an extra one: leaves that hide the golf ball. But once again, this is the old good-news, bad-news situation, for once the summer months are over, the rough thins out and becomes more manageable.

Just as you adjust for the condition of the trees and the rough based on the season, so you should account for the wind, which will also vary with the seasons. It can be gusty in early golfing weather, gentle in summer, sharp in the fall.

No matter what the season, wind is one of the great variables of golf. Wind conditions—the direction the wind is blowing, its velocity, and whether it is steady or intermittent—all do radical surgery on any golf plan that isn't flexible.

The weather, condition of the course, and the wind factor are among the items that should be on everyone's checklist. Some of these items you can review on your way to the course; the rest should be part of your pre-game warmup. How well you prepare can make a difference between being a casual golfer and a thoughtful one, and the difference is usually reflected on your scorecard.

One place where golfers consistently lose strokes isn't even

on the golf course; it is in the period between parking your car and teeing off on the first hole.

Two factors have a major influence on how well the golfer plays the first three or four holes, whether he is off to a good round, or whether he throws away strokes he can never retrieve:

- How much time the golfer spends warming up.
- How he utilizes his time.

Need proof? Just remember your last round. The chances are you scored much better on the back nine than the front. Most casual golfers do. The reason: after nine holes they're warmed up.

Meanwhile, of course, the round is half over. I ask you: Doesn't it make sense to warm up before the game rather than waste strokes warming up later?

Getting properly warmed up is one of the most important factors that go into an improved game of golf, its most obvious reasons being to loosen up the kinks and prevent injury.

Warming up isn't unique to golfers. Baseball players, football players, and athletes in all sports take time to loosen up before going into action. Unfortunately, too many golfers don't follow that common-sense approach.

The average golfer "cheats" on his preliminaries. He rarely allows time for preparation. Yet the weekend golfer in particular needs to warm up. He hasn't touched a club in a week, his concentration is lax, his body isn't ready, and his techniques are not in tune.

It isn't easy to budget that extra time. In my touring days I'd get to the course two hours early, relax for a half hour, then go out and hit fifty balls to warm up even before I went to the practice green. Now I rarely have time for that kind of full warmup.

These days I'm more likely to cut the practice time to forty-five minutes or an hour, and if I'm not careful I find myself

falling into worse habits—jumping out of the car, slipping on a pair of golf shoes, and heading for the first tee.

Invariably I pay a penalty of lost strokes, and I can't afford them any more than you can.

In short, there's a big difference between what you should do and what you can or will do. So if, despite all your good intentions, you arrive only moments before tee-off time, what can you do? The answer: Get your muscles moving.

- Do a few stretching exercises.
- Touch your toes.
- Do a few deep knee bends.
- Do a few twisting exercises to limber up your torso.

Let me give you a few pointers I've picked up by talking to experts in sports medicine. They say it is important to approach this limbering up process gradually.

You shouldn't try to stretch your muscles to capacity, nor should you "over-exercise." For example, avoid those "hurdler" exercises—you're going to play golf, not run the hurdles. Concentrate on your golf muscles.

It is your legs and torso that you want to loosen up. This phase of your preparation doesn't have to take a long time. Properly done, you can limit this part of your warmup to three minutes; five if you can.

Once you've gotten your body limbered up, you're off to a good start. But it is worth remembering that you are out to play a game of golf and that you've also got to limber up your golf swing.

I always try to hit a few balls before I play. If time is at a premium I'll throw down a couple of balls and hit them with an iron. Why an iron? It gives a better feel than a wood, and is more manageable.

You should always wind up your preliminaries with a few practice swings with your wood before you actually uncork your first drive.

However, this should never substitute for a good warmup,

and I'll stress that point again. The obvious shortcoming of the quickie warmup is that it is incomplete. It rushes you into your first shot too quickly and it shows.

You can usually tell from the first tee shot when a golfer has failed to warm up. One of the most common reasons why so many players push the first ball to the right or duck-hook is the failure to warm up their golf swing. They are tense, their muscles are tight, and because of their uncertainty they tend to rush the shot.

Another problem with the two-swings-and-away-we-go approach to golf is that it permits no time to map your strategy. Even more importantly, it fails to allow time for the practice putting green. It usually means that at least in the early part of the round you have to resort to pure guesswork in your putting. Invariably that costs strokes.

Let's face it, you rarely need to rush. Even if you're a last-minute golfer there are often delays on the first tee—sometimes enough to stretch your pre-game warmup to fifteen minutes. In that case I recommend splitting the time between full swings and putts, perhaps hitting five balls off the practice tee and then running over to try ten putts.

I think it is obvious that the best approach is to arrive at the golf course in plenty of time. Make it a point to get there about forty-five minutes early.

It also helps a lot if you are there by yourself, not with friends or opponents. There are no distractions and it permits you to concentrate solely on preparing your game.

It is my firm opinion that you should devote this practice period solely to preparing for the round you are about to start.

It is a common mistake to use this period to experiment. This is not the time to try out a new grip, a new stance, or a new club. It is too late. Experimenting will only add to your tensions. Instead, this is the time to ready the game you already have and, hopefully, put it all together.

Let's go back over a few pointers. Once you have gone through the brief stretching motions, the next task is to get your

golf swing loosened up. That's valid whether you have five minutes or two hours.

One handy aid for some players is a weighted club, a regular golf club that has been fitted with an extra-heavy head. Its advocates say it helps you feel the clubhead, and makes a single club feel lighter and more controllable when you pick it up.

I think the weighted club probably is a good exercise tool for the weekend golfer. It is likely that he hasn't hit any golf balls since his last game, and the heavier club accentuates his swing.

The weighted club can be especially helpful to the golfer who tends to rush his swing; unless you have exceptionally strong hands and wrists, it is very difficult to "hurry" the club.

I don't use the weighted club. When I have time, I often try a similar concept. I take two or three irons and swing them together in the same way in which you often see a baseball player take practice swings with several bats at a time. Most of my practice time, however, is spent hitting golf balls.

As a general rule, I start with the short irons and then work myself back to the driver—six or seven shots with a lofted iron, another half-dozen with a medium iron, a similar number with long irons, then a switch to fairway woods, and then the driver.

The objective of these practice shots is to develop a smooth swing; not necessarily a hard swing, but one that flows through the arc from backswing to follow-through. This is also a time to check your grip, your stance, and the "feel" of the club.

When I get to the long irons, I have developed a routine that I think you may find helpful. I hit the first shots off a tee, then hit the rest off the grass. Alternating between the tee and the ground involves a subtle change in the swing, and requires you to concentrate on the hitting area. It seems to help me "groove" my swing.

I usually devote half of my pregame warmup time to the irons and woods. Then I move to the putting green. Par golf is based on two putts per hole; the remaining strokes are those needed to get the golfer to the green. The green is also the "equalizer"—the place where a shorter-hitting golfer can catch up and even pass a longer but less accurate opponent.

The key to good putting is consistency, and consistency comes from rolling the ball toward the hole. A rolling putt runs to the hole smoothly. By contrast, a poorly struck putt bumps along.

How do you make the ball roll smoothly? The correct technique is to hit the ball with the putter face square both to the line to the hole and square from the ground up. (See Illustration #1.)

Good putting comes from practice. But when it comes to putting, I find most golfers don't know how to practice. Typically they drop a ball about twenty feet from the cup, lag one up, and then try to sink the second shot. Then they go on to the next twenty- or thirty-foot practice putts.

I can understand their thinking, but I disagree with it. They are trying to simulate the conditions they will face on the putting green. I think that is a mistake. Their concern should be getting the ball into the cup with two strokes; no more. To do that, they need to practice their putting. But first they need to improve it.

What you learn over the years is that it isn't the thirty- and forty-foot birdie putts that make a good golfer; it is the ability to avoid taking an unnecessary number of putts.

The way the higher handicap player learns to improve his putting scores is by dividing his strokes on the green into two parts (See Illustration #2):

- Mastering the technique of getting the ball within a three-foot range on the initial putt.
- Learning to sink the short ones.

The place to start is with the short, "gimme" putts—one foot, eighteen inches, two feet. Don't move back until you are totally confident you can sink the putt most of the time. Then gradually work back to three feet. If you can meet the challenge of the short putts, you're halfway on the road to becoming a master of the greens.

It is important, however, to be aware of the proper techniques of putting. It is possible that on a given day you will

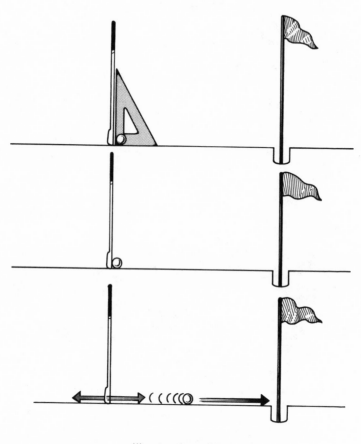

Illustration #1

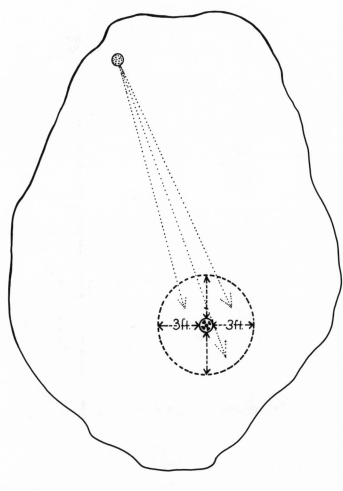

Illustration #2

sink your short putts even though you are doing a lot of things incorrectly. You discover the problem the next time out, when those same putts simply do not fall.

I think the answer is to first concentrate on rolling the ball. Accuracy will follow. The really good players putt consistently because they roll the ball and roll it the same way, whether in a three-foot or a sixty-foot putt. (See Illustration #3.)

We've defined a short putt as one of up to three feet from the cup. When you get beyond that point, your perspective must change. From three feet to ten feet, your efforts should be directed toward getting the ball as close to the hole as possible, for a tap-in.

From ten feet away your goal is fixed: no more than two putts per green. Under no circumstance do you want to take a gamble that may leave you more than three feet from the cup.

For putts of ten feet or more your objective is to lag the ball up to a point where you can get down in two every time. That means taking no more than two strokes to get the ball into the three-foot circle where you have just been practicing.

If you become proficient enough to get your approach putt into "sure" territory, you will find your odds are improving. Not only will you increase your chances of getting down in par figures, but as a bonus, every once in a while one of those lag putts will wind up in the hole.

We've set these goals for the average golfer, but the same guidelines apply to the better golfer. He too should concentrate on bringing his longer putts to within tap-in range, but should be able to expand more quickly to a target area larger than three feet, and should be able to sink a greater percentage of those ten- and twenty-footers.

Distance is always far more important than anything else in putting because you can tell at a glance which is the high side and how much it will break. But it is the distance that will determine how close you get that putt. The really good putters always control the distance; there are days in which they may miss one side or the other, but they roll the ball for distance consistently.

Illustration #3

Since your objective is to get the ball as close to the hole as possible, you want to avoid hitting it too hard, too softly, or so off-line that it ends up outside your three-foot target area.

In most cases the best way to do this is to "go for it." Unless the green is a complicated maze of plateaus, peaks, and valleys, you can usually take direct aim at the hole rather than trying to determine the exact path of the ball. Make a slight adjustment in your line, if you must, on the "high" side. But if there are any doubts in your mind, shoot straight for the cup.

Remember that you are seeking the proper distance, not the miracle putt. If you've got the distance right, the slant of the green isn't going to leave you far from the hole.

After you've worked on your lag putts, I suggest moving off the green and doing a little work on your chip shots. Again, the goal is the same: to send the ball the right distance, so that it winds up within the three-foot circle and you are left with only a short final putt.

Once you've worked your way through the warmup I've just outlined, you'll probably be getting close to tee-off time. Now is the time for the final limbering up. At this point I recommend that you complete your warmup with a few swings with a middle-range iron, then a long iron, and finally take a few hefty swings with your driving wood.

If you have followed the procedures I've recommended, you should be warmed up and have a feel for the greens, with your hands golf-strong and your body limbered up. You should now be ready to go with your confidence firmly in place.

Warming up before starting a round of golf is a lot easier for the pro than for the amateur. Among other things, golf is the business of a pro and he knows the importance of preparation. Perhaps even more important, limbering up really isn't optional for the pro; it is part of the regular tournament routine.

Without question, the major difference between my days on the pro tour and the golf I play today is the shorter warmup time before I take my first shot off the tee. For the pro, practice

41

time is almost automatic. When you're in tournament play, everything revolves around your tee time.

On the other hand, the amateur has many demands on his time. Business, family, and personal matters usually have a higher priority than getting to the golf course, even for a crucial game. And even if there is a tee-off time, it is often fairly flexible.

Topping this off, most casual golfers allow just enough time to play golf. They are usually too impatient to spend time practicing, and even if they do, they find it isn't easy to discipline themselves into making the pre-game warmup a "must."

By contrast, the pro has few options. Most professionals feel that we really have to work hard at our game if we're going to play well. If golf is your living, and if you don't play well, you don't make the cut and you wind up with no paycheck.

Too many experiences like this and you're no longer in the golfing business.

What it boils down to is that most pro golfers have a set routine just as rigid as that of the guy with the 9-to-5 job downtown.

There is pretty much a set schedule for all tournaments. With the notable exception of the Bob Hope Desert Classic, which runs five days, pro tournaments start on a Thursday and run four days. Typically, the pro golfer finishes one tournament on a Sunday and plans to arrive at the next tournament city on the following day, Monday, perhaps by car or plane, depending upon the tour and the distances.

Tuesday is normally a working day. It is a day set aside for taking a look at the golf course. Most players plan a practice round. If you've played the course before, you want to review it. If it is new to you, you have a chance to get acquainted.

On Tuesday afternoon the golfers are notified of their Thursday and Friday tee-off times. In the United States the selection of starting times is called "the pairings"—pairing up the golfers who will play together. In England and Australia, they call it the "draw"—because, in theory, the names are drawn out of a hat.

Here's how it works. Most tournaments start around 8 o'clock in the morning. The exceptions are California tournaments in January; those are started as early as possible because it is difficult to get all players through before dark.

Of the 150 players, half will play early on Thursday and half will play early on Friday. The players go out in threesomes approximately eight minutes apart, so the so-called afternoon round usually starts around 11:30 A.M.

There are a number of ways your threesome and tee-off time is determined. When I was on the tour, all players were divided into three categories. The consistent money winners got the best starting times—around nine in the morning or one in the afternoon.

Players who had won tournaments during the past three years got the next best times and the newcomers or the players who weren't doing so well drew the earliest and latest starting times. Within each of those three categories, the individual threesomes were picked by lot.

Once you learn your starting time for Thursday and Friday, your schedule for the week starts to fit into place.

Wednesday is the day of the pro-amateur tournament. If you are one of the top forty money winners of the previous year, you play; if not, you're excluded and either try to get in a few holes before the first tee-off or you do your golf homework on the practice green or driving range.

Not every eligible player competes in the pro-am. You can cancel one in every four of these tourneys if you choose, but that's not commonly done. For one thing, the pro-am is important to the tournament; it helps raise money.

In the pro-am, each pro teams up with a foursome of amateurs. Because each of the four amateurs pays from $700 to $2,000 to play, it is possible for a pro-am tournament to raise more than a quarter of a million dollars. That's a lot of encouragement for tournament sponsors!

It is also important to the individual pro. It costs a lot of money to go on tour. The entry fee was only $25 for many of the early tournaments I played in, and it really hasn't gone up

that much since then. But a professional golfer has the same kind of expenses any traveling person would have—plane fares, hotel bills, and meals, as well as caddie fees.

Even a bare-bones budget likely will exceed $2,500 per tournament, and unless you're among the top money winners, you won't be able to make out with the money you collect in tournament prizes alone.

Fortunately there are opportunities to make money other than by placing in the rankings in tournaments. Many pro-am tournaments pay the pro for his appearance. There are also exhibitions, clothing, and ball contracts that can add up. The year I was seventy-fourth on the money list, I made about $62,000 in outside income. For a top player like Tom Watson, side money will be many times over what he gets in tournament winnings.

Besides the purses put up for the tournament itself, there is prize money in the pro-am competition. The amateurs play with their handicap, and the best score among the four is combined with that of the pro to constitute a best-ball tournament. There is a separate competition among the pros.

But while whatever money you can win in the pro-am is important, the big advantage in being able to compete is the chance to play the course right before the tournament, and play it under competitive circumstances.

That really gives you a chance to become familiar with the course before the big money is at stake.

After the first tournament round on Thursday and the second round on Friday, it is cutdown time, and more than half the players are eliminated. Of 150 players who tee off in the competition, only the top seventy (and any tied players) remain. If you don't make the cut you have a long weekend and no paycheck.

Until a few years ago the penalty for missing the cut was even more drastic. The player who missed was not only eliminated from the competition, but unless exempt, he wasn't eligible for the next tournament either.

The only way to play was to qualify all over again. This

meant playing on a Monday, and was often a tough challenge—eighteen holes of competition, sometimes for only five
or six open spots.

Sometimes you got lucky, however, and the exempt players
failed to exercise their options. As a result, some tournaments
had as many as twenty or thirty openings. Even so, it normally
took par golf, or close to it, to make the qualifying cutoff.

That ordeal was tough on the nerves, the pocketbook, and
the morale and—wisely I think—the PGA changed the rules in
1982 to eliminate the practice of requiring some golfers to
qualify for individual tournaments. They also expanded the
number of exempted players on the tour.

Instead of exempting only sixty top money winners, the list
was increased to 125. This didn't freeze out new golfers; the
route I took to get my card is still open. In fact there may be
room for even more newcomers if some of the PGA's plans for
breaking the tour into two segments materialize—half playing
one week, the other half the next, and coming together only for
the Masters, Open, and a few of the other top prestige competi-
tions.

Dropping the qualifying system probably has made it difficult, perhaps impossible, for a player like myself to come back
for an occasional tournament. But for the player who wants to
take a full shot at the pro tour, it will eliminate some of the
heartbreaks of the past, and I'm all for it.

The tournament season lasts forty weeks, knocking off from
the end of October through Christmas, but most players don't
stick to it week-in and week-out; it is too easy to lose your
game if you hold too tight a schedule.

As a matter of fact, in my opinion that's the main reason Arnold Palmer no longer is a dominant player. Palmer blames it
on his putting, but I think that in the days when he was on top,
he played so many times for so many years that he probably
burned himself out. He simply doesn't have the sharp, keen
game he had when he was playing his competitive best.

I don't think that will happen to Jack Nicklaus; he picks his
spots. Tom Watson is trying to do the same.

What slows any golfer down are injuries. Quite a number of pro golfers develop back problems, the kind that forced Jack Nicklaus out of the 1983 Masters. Sam Snead never lost that incredibly smooth swing, but as he got older he found the ball didn't go as far. Among some senior golfers, the legs start to give. But probably the clearest sign that a golfer is in danger of going downhill is in his putting.

For younger players, overplaying the game can be a serious problem. It is customary for the tour players to take about ten weeks off every year. Most pros play in thirty of the forty tournaments; the stars will play between twenty and twenty-five.

Sometimes a player will skip a tournament because he doesn't like a course. For many years Lee Trevino refused to play at the Masters because he didn't like the golf course.

More recently, Calvin Peete got some negative publicity for the same reason. He also said he didn't like the course, but what he was really saying was that his game was not well suited to the course. He played anyway, but didn't do well.

A lot of golfers and a lot of golf courses are not suited to each other. The long-ball hitter has an edge on a wide-open course, but can run into trouble on a course that demands precision.

The reverse is also true; the player whose strong suit is accuracy may simply not have the distance to play competitively against the big boomers. It is also true that some golfers will badmouth a course simply because they have played it poorly before.

In most cases in which a pro runs into that kind of trouble, however, it is likely to be a sign that he is "golfed out"; that he has lost his sense of dedication and feels stale. He doesn't have the concentration power needed to tackle the many challenges every golf course presents.

Losing your enthusiasm is a sure sign that you're losing your competitive edge. When that happened to me, I wouldn't go near a golf course. Instead I'd play hooky from practice and check out a few movies.

A more serious problem occurs when something fundamen-

tal to your game goes sour. For example, there are times when you develop a bug in your swing. That usually requires special treatment. Another pro can sometimes spot the difficulty for you: some minor flaw that has crept into your swing.

Frequently, however, it won't respond to the "quick fix." Trying to locate and correct a defect in the swing on a Wednesday, one day before a tournament, is like cramming for a final examination on the night before. It rarely works.

Sometimes you can play your way out of a problem, but that's risky. You may simply be reinforcing bad golf habits. Most tour players find it best to take time out to locate the flaw and find a way to repair it.

The average player who confines his golf to weekend play has some of these problems. True, he doesn't get enough playing time over the golfing season to get stale. But he can suffer from indifference. He can lack the drive it takes to play his best at all times. He can have trouble with his golfing concentration.

It is worth remembering that every player has golfing problems at some time or another. The real question is "what to do" about those problems. The weekender will be tempted to try to stretch his limited golfing time and seek a cure for his shortcomings by experimenting during a round. I don't think that works for a pro or serious amateur.

The time to work on fundamentals is during practice.

Let me define what I mean by "practice." I mean time devoted solely to practice and experimentation. Specifically, it means you don't practice when you're playing a round or during your pregame warmup. When you want to practice that's all you do, practice.

You can pick up a pointer from the pros. The best time for a touring pro to practice is after he has played a round of golf. Your golfing problems are fresh in your mind. The pressures of the day are behind you. In the case of the pro, he has up to twenty-four hours before his next tee time, and even the non-pro is likely to have some free time after a round to work on his game.

Rather than going to the "nineteenth hole" to brood over the missed shots and mistakes of the day, why not try it the professional way: Put in a little time on the putting green or practice tee. It will pay dividends in next week's outing.

Later on we'll talk more about spotting errors and how to correct them. For the time being we want to concentrate on your golf thinking. We're not going to try to change your game; we're going to take your present game and make it better through improved strategy.

We will consider golf in three stages: getting warmed up for a game, playing a round of golf, and finally improving your swing. We've talked about warming up; now let's "warm up" our golf thinking.

Pro golfers work on their golf strategy on the course itself. The practice round is where the pro prepares his game, which is why most of us try to work in at least one practice round before a tournament.

A practice round is just what its title suggests—a chance to practice. I've already pointed out that you shouldn't practice in the pregame warmup or during a round. For the same reason, it is usually counterproductive to play for money during the practice round; you're likely to concentrate on winning rather than learning.

Do just one thing at a time. If you're going to warm up, warm up. If you're going to play a round of golf, play a round of golf. If you're going to practice, practice.

The pro-am tournament is somewhat different. It is played under tournament conditions and you play to win, but like the practice session it should also come under the label of "preparation." You should know a lot more about the course after you finish the round, not just what your score was.

Practice rounds are somewhat informal. The pro goes out to the tee and waits for others who want to play, so that, just as in a weekend round, he can become part of a foursome.

As you know, a golfer is not allowed to confer with anyone but his caddie during a tournament. But in a practice round

there is always conversation about the course and how it plays. It is partly shop talk, but it is also educational.

When I'm in competition, I try to completely block out my playing partner or fellow competitor and his game. I want to concentrate solely on my own game and the golf course. But the practice round doesn't require that singlemindedness.

On the contrary, it can be a good idea to be observant. It is an opportunity to see how another player tackles a given hole. If I'm playing a draw and somebody else is playing a cut shot, I want to find out what happens to his shot. He may have a better idea than I have, especially on a hole where I'm having trouble.

I'm also interested in seeing how the ball reacts to the way he hits it. It is as true in golf as in anything else that you can always learn if you want to.

There is another practical reason to keep an open mind: Conditions on a golf course can change. My shot may be the right one for now, but the other guy's tactic may be the answer to a different situation later in the tournament, when wind or weather alters the way the hole plays.

The practice round should be a learning experience and, if there is time, a chance to try some alternative strategies. When I play a shot, I know where I want it to go. But it doesn't always work the way I planned it. So besides playing my game ball, I may hit a second ball from the spot where I wanted the game ball to land. Hopefully that is the shot I will hit in competition.

It may be worth taking several varied shots to find the right one for a given hole; since I'm only tuning up my game, the score is meaningless; it is the tournament scores that count.

A number of factors will determine how the practice round is utilized. For example, if I have just finished a tournament in San Antonio and am getting ready for competition in San Francisco, I will be facing new greens. Instead of the Bermuda grass of Texas, I will be putting on bent grass. I will spend a lot of time on the practice green, even before a practice round. I will pay particular attention to each green and how it "reads."

If I know the course, my routine will differ. Since most tournaments are held at the same golf courses year in and year out, the tour veteran rarely faces a brand-new challenge. I carry scorecards and yardage books from previous rounds. And while I don't keep a shot-by-shot record (although that would be a good idea), I do have a basic plan for playing the course.

What I need to know is whether there are any innovations. There are a few golf courses where they are always experimenting. I remember the Tucson National where they always seemed to be tinkering with the layout. Occasionally a course will revamp or alter a hole. But most times the changes aren't radical. In any event it pays to be observant. A trap may have been shortened or lengthened; a tee relocated. Each change is likely to require some adjustment in your game plan. Even the loss or addition of a single tree can make a hole play entirely different.

But whether it is a new course or one you've played before, there is really only one thing that changes: the driving area. That's where I devote most of my pre-tournament attention.

What do I mean by driving area? I mean the target circle of the fairway where I want my drive to stop.

A number of factors are involved in choosing the driving area. Normally you'd like to pick out an area as far and as straight as possible ahead of the tee. But that's not always the right target.

In some instances the correct target will be an area to which I'm forced to shoot by special concerns prompted by the course itself or the characteristics of my game. An out-of-bounds area may alter my strategy. If my drives are hooking more than usual, I may shift my target area.

It is imperative to pick the right target area. The one thing I don't want to do is hit a good shot and find that it was a mistake. Or hit a good shot and find that it could have been better. Let me illustrate this.

It is entirely possible to hit a drive straight down the middle of the fairway. That normally would be considered a good golf shot. But if it leaves you with an unusually difficult second

shot to the green, it could prove a mistake. A shot aimed to the right or left to "open up" the green would probably have been a better selection.

The answer to seek out during a practice round is: On this particular hole on this particular course and under these particular circumstances, what is the best target area for my game?

My preparation also includes a study of the scorecard. This is a good habit for every golfer to get into, particularly when playing a strange course. You never know what you may find. I remember one hole in the Canadian Open at Glen Abbey in Oakville, Ontario. The situation was unusual, a crosswalk in the driving area. Apparently there was no other convenient passage for spectators who wanted to move to another part of the course.

The walk was deep grass and many of the players were deliberately laying up short of it to avoid trouble. But I had learned that the Tournament Players Association had issued a special ruling that made the crosswalk a free drop.

Under the rule, you were permitted to drop the ball in front of the walk if your shot landed in that area. Knowing that rule gave me a chance to try to drive to the walkway instead of playing short. I was gambling on a sure thing.

The scorecard gives the yardage on every hole. That helps plan your club selection. Some cards will even contain miniature maps of each hole and some landmarks to assist in judging distances.

In tournament competition there is another aid—the yardage book, made by some enterprising person who visits the course in advance and prepares a detailed map of it. The yardage book marks off all the distances from sprinkler heads to the green. The regular scorecard lists the distance from tee to green, but that's not really important to the pro. He needs to know the in-between distances. Off the tee the golfer wants to know distance to a given trap so he will know what he has to do to carry it. Say it is 258 yards to the trap and 272 yards to carry the trap. Then you'd know you could hit a 3-wood and not go in the trap but you couldn't carry it even if you hit with a driver.

Other than the tee shot, the pro wants to know distances to the green. These days most courses have automatic sprinkler systems and they are consistently spaced, usually either 25 or 30 yards apart. The yardage book marks off the distance from any given sprinkler to the front edge of the green.

The book also provides the various distances on the putting green so you can have guidelines on which to base your shot depending on where the cup is placed that particular day.

The yardage book usually costs about $10, and it is invaluable. I make notes in it as I take my practice round, and then make sure to tuck it into my golf bag. I don't want to take a chance of forgetting it; during a tournament the yardage book will be consulted on almost every one of the seventy-two holes.

In theory, I suppose you could even plot your strategy from the yardage book. That's not my approach, however. Golf is more than a game of just-so-many-yards from tee to green. I think you have to do your planning by ''feel,'' since a course can change into many different courses as a result of the weather, playing conditions, and time of day.

It is only from the experience of playing a course that you know how the ball will react under different circumstances. For example, if you have been using a 3-wood on a given hole and you're suddenly facing a fifteen-mile-an-hour wind, you know you can safely use a driver without overshooting your target. Or if the wind shifts downwind from tee to green, you can scale back to a 4-wood or a long iron.

Whether in regular play, casual play, or a practice round, it is smart golf to play one shot at a time and one hole at a time. Even when playing a strange course, I can't concern myself with any hole other than the one that I'm playing at the moment. I strongly recommend that you take the same attitude.

Now, before we tee up for our first shot, let's review briefly.

Check out anything that can influence how the course plays. What time of year is it? Golf courses reflect the seasons just as private lawns do. What kind of a day is it going to be? What

has the weather been recently and how could it affect the greens and fairways?

What time of day is it? Early dew slows the greens. Traffic plays a toll as the day goes on, drying the greens and making it more difficult to control the ball. Are the fairways recently cut or sprinkled? Are the sand traps freshly raked or packed hard? How tall is the rough?

Is there a wind? How strong is it blowing and in what direction? Is it likely to shift during the round or change in velocity? Make a mental note to check the direction of each hole from tee to green and how the wind will influence your shot.

On most courses the holes change direction. You may be shooting with the wind on one hole, be facing a quartering wind on the next, and be playing into the wind on the third. The wide-awake player keeps track of this and accounts for the wind in planning his shots.

Study the scorecard and, on a strange course, note any local rules. Take a look to see if the scorecard identifies directions. This can help you orient yourself to the wind direction on each hole.

Before playing, warm up your muscles. When you arrive in the tee area, follow the routine we discussed earlier. Take three to five minutes to do easy stretching exercises to get your leg and torso muscles active.

Limber up your golf swing with your irons, then move to your fairway woods and driving wood.

Split your time between the fairway clubs and the putter.

In putting, start with twelve-inch putts until you roll the ball well, then work until you sink those one-foot putts and, more importantly, sink them consistently; then gradually move back to a three-foot distance. Regardless of the length of your putts, concentrate on developing a dependable roll to each. Work from all angles so you test out the variations in the green.

On the longer putts, concentrate on distance. Aim for the three-foot circle around the hole where you feel confident of sinking the putt.

Don't experiment with your game. Go with what you've got, at least for now.

Get yourself ready, physically and mentally.

Now let's head for the tee.

Chapter 3

Teeing off
With Confidence

Probably no shot in golf is harder to put into the proper perspective than the drive off the first tee.

The average golfer gives it too much importance. He permits the initial tee shot to set his mood for the day. If it is a good shot, he isn't quite sure just why it came off well and tends to attribute it to luck. If it is a bad shot, it makes him doubt his game. Either way, he starts second-guessing himself even as he walks off the tee.

There is too much to golf to allow any single shot to have that strong an influence on your game. It is considerably more productive—and more realistic—to understand that the first shot is important but not crucial.

I can remember only one tournament that may have been lost on the first shot of the round. I was playing in a National Junior Chamber of Commerce tournament in Waterloo, Iowa, and one of the outstanding juniors in the country, Marty Fleckman, was also competing.

If you've been following golf for some time, the name Marty Fleckman may ring a bell. He led the 1967 National Open at Baltusrol through the first three rounds. He had an opening 67, then a 73 and a 69, and going into the final round, he was one stroke ahead of Jack Nicklaus, Billy Casper, and Arnold Palmer.

Fleckman ran into trouble on the fourth round. He pushed three shots out to the right, each requiring a recovery shot back onto the fairway. His putter also deserted him, and when the round was over he had a 38-42 for an 80, and with it the end of his dream to be the first amateur to win the Open since Johnny Goodman did it in 1933.

But Fleckman was probably doomed anyway. Nicklaus got hot on the fourth round and burned up the course with a 65 for a record-breaking 275 for the tournament.

But Fleckman kept his sense of humor. He told reporters that he had found his "real" golf game at Baltusrol. On the fourth round. And he even joked about it, saying "It took me four days to get back on my game, but I finally made it."

At the time of the Junior Chamber tournament at Waterloo, Marty was only seventeen, but was already one of the top young amateurs, and had a real chance to win it.

The course was a "tight" one without much room for error. On the first tee, Fleckman drove the ball out of bounds. He teed up again and promptly hit his second drive out of bounds. He then hit a third drive and this too went out of bounds.

All three shots were almost identical—off line to the left. Finally, on his fourth try, the ball stayed in play. Each of those out-of-bounds shots had cost him two shots, one stroke for the drive and one shot for penalty. By the time he left the tee Fleckman was already on his seventh shot.

Down six strokes, most players would have folded. You can't expect to give the rest of the field a half-dozen strokes and still remain competitive. For Fleckman, making the cut alone meant making up his deficit in two rounds.

By any standard it was a long shot, and winning was out of the question.

But that didn't stop Marty Fleckman. He played extremely well the rest of the day and shot a 76, which would have been an under-par 70 without those lost strokes. The second day he shot a 70 and made the cut handily. On the third day he shot a 73 and on the final day a 71.

He didn't win the tournament. His four-round total was 290.

The winner, Ray Floyd, had 284. The difference was three out-of-bounds tee shots.

But Marty Fleckman's misfortune is an unusual example of a tournament which was really decided on the first tee. In most cases, the first tee shot is neither more nor less important than any other.

I speak from experience. Over the years I've hit thousands of golf balls. I've hit my share of shots into Nowhere and I've hit some super shots on the first tee. Still, I can't say that hitting a good or bad shot to open a round meant that I was going to have a good or bad day.

However, I'd much rather start out with a good shot.

There are poker players who think it is bad luck to win the first pot. And it is an old baseball superstition that striking out the first batter is a jinx. Maybe so, but in golf I think there's nothing like getting off to a good start with your first drive.

Among other things, a good first drive helps you remember some of the great days. I can recall the time I shot a 66 at White Marsh Country Club in Philadelphia—one of those courses built near the turn of the century, with narrow fairways: a tight, demanding layout.

The first hole was only 350 yards and the fairway only about 20 yards wide. I hit a superdrive that carried to within sixty yards of the green. It was a sensational start and my day turned bright and stayed that way.

Starting off well does give your spirits a shot of adrenaline. As a matter of fact, if I were designing my ideal golf course, the first hole would be an easy par-3. That would give you a better-than-even chance to get off to a good start.

The trouble is that there aren't many courses like that. In all my travels, I can only remember one course where the first hole was a par-3. That was Pleasant Valley in Sutton, Massachusetts. For some reason, the tournament committee at the Pleasant Valley Classic decided to reverse the two halves of the course and made the tenth hole the tee-off hole.

As I recall, it was an elevated tee and an elevated green, but a downhill fairway about 165 yards long, and most players

used a 6-, 7-, or 8-iron. I thought it provided an interesting start to a golf round.

In almost every instance, however, the first hole is a par-4 or a par-5, and you face a challenge right from the time you walk up to the tee.

There is a practical reason for that design. If the course started with a par-3 hole, a foursome playing the hole would have to hole out before the next foursome could play out, and things would get pretty jammed up around the first green on the course—a very effective way to get golfers mad at a course.

As a player, I would find it interesting to start out with a par-3 hole, but I'm not sure it would really work to relieve all those anxieties to which golfers are prone. Whether the hole is long or short, no one completely escapes the sense of uncertainty about how that first tee shot will turn out.

Let's face it. The initial shot of the day *is* tough.

In theory, it shouldn't be all that troublesome. That first tee shot isn't the most difficult one you'll face during a round of golf.

As a matter of fact, from a technical viewpoint, the initial shot on any golf course is usually relatively easy. You have a choice of where to place your ball, its lie is perfect (a tee), and on most golf courses, the first hole is one of the least demanding of the eighteen.

By contrast, at some point on the course you'll have a tight lie, an obstructing tree branch, a tricky putt—all of them a greater challenge to your golfing ability than the demands of the first drive.

Why then is the first shot on the first tee such an awesome experience? Partly because the initial effort in any sport is challenging. The first pitch in a baseball game, the first football play from scrimmage, the first blow in a prize fight—all have the same impact. Each signals that the preliminaries are over and now it's for real.

Golf has another factor: psychology. Golf is a physical sport, but hitting a golf ball for the first time on any given day is really more of a mental challenge.

This is why the first tee shot is where most golfers make their first mistake of the round, letting their doubts get between themselves and the clubhead.

The problem isn't in the golfer's game, but in his head, and the remedy—as it is so often in golf—is to avoid mental errors. And probably the worst of such mental errors is uncertainty. Having doubts undermines your confidence.

If I start out with confidence, I nearly always play better golf. I don't mean confidence of the sort that says I'm going to burn up the course or am suddenly going to find some magic to conquer a course where I normally have trouble; I mean confidence in the sense that I'm not going to start out with doubts about myself and my game. I'm not going to beat myself even before I begin play.

Let me give you some examples.

If you've been spraying your drives all over the lot either in practice or during recent rounds, you can have plenty of trouble with your first drive. You will have a tendency to tense up. You'll have a bit of fear in your swing.

You really don't have confidence that the ball will go where you want it to.

Under that kind of pressure, there's a great temptation to try to steer the ball into the fairway. That almost always brings bad news. The odds are that you will wind up either topping it or pulling it to the left.

Take the golfer with a pronounced slice. He is prone to try to correct his problem on the first tee, and is so worried about the slice he doesn't remember to hit the ball.

Regardless of his ability, a golfer who goes to the tee with a lot of uncertainty is undercutting his odds for a decent shot. He is substantially reducing the likelihood that he will get off to a good start in his round of golf.

Obviously the place to work out these doubts is in your warmup. The golfer who doesn't warm up is particularly vulnerable. He doesn't feel comfortable. He is not yet prepared physically, and consciously or unconsciously, he knows it and tightens up.

By contrast, if you hit some good shots in your pregame practice, you'll walk to the first tee with much greater self confidence. Achieving that feeling of confidence should be one of your aims in the pregame ritual. Hit enough shots with your driving wood so that, with as much accuracy as possible, you can predict just what is going to happen to the ball when you hit it.

Professional golfers have an expression: "Play within yourself." It means to play the game of which you are capable. Know your capabilities and your limitations. Learn to play within yourself.

Once you have learned how to correctly assess your abilities, you have the basis for building confidence in your game. And when you gain confidence, your game automatically improves.

In my own case, the better I play, the more confidence I get in my game, and it shows up particularly on the first tee. I had one stretch on the tour in 1978 in which my golf was so consistent that I developed supreme trust in my game.

The place where that confidence was most evident was on my initial drive. Not too surprisingly, the first tee shot in those months felt no different than any other. I didn't always hit the perfect drive, but I felt sure it would be a good one—and by golly, more often than not it was.

Everybody would like to get a good drive off the first tee. Unfortunately, as I've already noted, too many golfers are tempted to regard a good drive as a long one. They try for extra distance on the theory that it will bring them closer to the green quicker, and get them off to a par or birdie start.

All too often that determination to "let out the shaft" results in a pressed shot that starts the golfer out in trouble, and with it, those same old doubts start creeping in—again unnecessarily.

Haste is another common fault on the first tee. Most golfers are too impatient. New players, in particular, feel they are "on stage." They are insecure and want to get that first shot over with as quickly as possible.

My grandmother used to say "haste makes waste." She wasn't a golfer, but the expression is apt. A rushed shot usually winds up topped, shanked, or pulled because the player is not in good balance. He doesn't have the smooth tempo you need for a good shot.

The confident golfer has to have the proper objective. Everybody would like to get off a good first drive, but it is important to know what constitutes a good drive. You have to know what you're trying to do.

Let me re-emphasize that distance is not the prime consideration in golf. When a golfer tries for distance, he tends to overdo himself. What a smart golfer should be seeking is a shot that carries well, but more significantly, lands the ball in a good spot. That's the kind of leadoff stroke that gives you the feeling that your swing is in the groove and under control.

This is what we talked about earlier when we discussed hitting the "target zone" with your tee shot.

How do you do that?

First, let's take a look at the club you're using. If you are like most golfers, your choice is your driver, the Number-1 wood. It is the club with the greatest potential for distance. It is also one of the most difficult clubs to master.

Unless you are a low-handicap player, I suggest you put away the driver and pull out a Number-2 wood for your tee shots. It is a more lofted club. It gets the ball into the air, and for a great many amateurs getting the ball airborne is one of the most difficult parts of the game.

Not only is the 2-wood better at getting your drive off the ground, it is also easier to develop confidence in this club. The shaft is shorter and the clubface is cut back that extra bit that seems to make it simpler to hit the ball squarely. To a great extent, that advantage is in your mind, but that's exactly where you want it—where it is adding to your self-confidence.

It isn't all mental, however. You can hit a better shot with a 2-wood than with a driver. If you make an error in your swing, you will get a twenty-percent better result with a 2-wood than you would with a driver. That's a pretty good reason to make

the switch. You may even choose to drive with a 3-wood. The difference is only about 15 yards.

If you have the right club and the proper confidence, you have two key ingredients to a good first tee shot. There is a third factor that is probably the most obvious, but is commonly overlooked.

You have to know where you are going to hit the ball.

When you get to the first tee, you have a number of alternatives; a number of things that can happen to your ball when you hit your drive. Let's rank them in order, starting with the best.

Ideally you'll put the ball out there where you planned. The best place is on the fairway. And the best place on the fairway is where you have a good lie and the opportunity for a good second shot. If you could do that consistently, you would be playing championship golf.

Even the best players don't have that much control, and not every shot stays in the fairway. It doesn't necessarily follow that every shot in the fairway is desirable either; as we'll discuss later, some fairway shots are very troublesome.

In general, however, your top priority is to keep the ball in the fairway. If you can't, your next highest priority is to at least get it in the short rough. True, the ball is harder to control from the rough than from the fairway. If you have to play your second shot out of the short rough, your accuracy will suffer.

But there are worse places to be, especially for less-than-expert golfers.

A shot that is usually even less desirable than a shot from the rough is one from a fairway bunker. The average golfer feels less comfortable in sand than he does in the rough, and is likely to have trouble with his swing.

So unless there is a low lip on the trap and a decent lie, most golfers are going to have to use a more lofted club, and that costs yardage. Even under ideal circumstances the ball has so much spin when hit from a fairway bunker that you lose about one club's worth of distance.

On the other hand, traps around the green are more or less comparable to shots out of the rough, particularly if you're rea-

sonably adept at handling them. If not, they're usually tougher than a shot from the rough.

Further down in the second-shot category are positions that really hurt. These are the shots where you can't get a decent chance to hit the ball. They are typically shots that almost always cost you a shot in order to recover. Examples are a ball under bushes, up against a tree, or in a spot in the woods from which it is virtually impossible to escape.

Worse yet are the shots that land in a water hazard and wind up costing you a stroke. In this group also are topping the ball or whiffing—errors that don't advance the ball but use up a stroke.

Rounding out the bad-news department is the out-of-bounds shot, which costs a stroke and distance.

Once you have gone through the list of problem shots, it is time to put the information to work. The best way is to create a "caution file" in your mind. Give the highest caution rating to out-of-bounds shots because they create your most costly penalties.

You must treat a water hazard with similar respect.

Don't overdo the process, however. It is very important to think positively and to plan your game as you see it rather than overemphasize the potential for trouble.

In general, I think you can usually tell at a glance which problem areas you can afford to ignore and which you must respect. Once you have singled out the hazards that merit your concern, there are some simple steps to take.

Normally, you should tee up on the side of the trouble area. For example, if the out-of-bounds area is on the left, tee up on the left side of the tee area.

Second, if there is a water hazard, evaluate just how significant its location is. If any kind of decent shot will avoid the hazard, forget it and worry about something else. A hazard is a problem only if you land in it.

On the other hand, if there is a reasonable chance that your shot might land in the water, see if there is a way to minimize its dangers. For instance, if there's a chance that trying a shot in one direction could put you into a water hazard, and the al-

ternative shot might leave you in the rough, take the one with the lesser penalty. That's playing percentages.

Once you have made up your mind, you are usually ready to try your shot. But don't rush. If you feel tense and uncertain, take time to walk away and try a few loosening-up swings. Then try again.

Too many golfers want to get the shot over with, apparently on the assumption that it is best to get it done and hope for the best. In my experience, hope doesn't help much on the golf course. You're a lot better off taking a few extra minutes to get control of your shot.

Finally, after you have hit the shot, start planning your next one. As you walk down the fairway begin to take in your surroundings. Where did your ball land? What are your alternatives in approaching the green?

It is futile to either admire a good shot or curse a bad one. Both are past history, and brooding over a bad shot or bad luck robs you of the concentration you need to play well.

Remember once again that luck has a tendency to even out, if you let it. Good play tends to overcome bad, if you try.

We've been talking about planning your game around the hazards on the golf course, and have made the point that you usually play your best game if you can keep the ball consistently in the fairway. But where in the fairway?

As we said earlier, you have to know where you're going to hit the ball.

It boils down to this: How can you ever hit the ball if you don't know where you want to hit it? There is a big difference between aiming for a certain part of the golf course and aiming at the world.

All too often, high-handicap players aim at the world.

If this is your problem, what can you do about it? I think you have to develop a picture in your mind of the path the ball will travel after you hit it. I have found one of the best ways to visualize a drive or long fairway shot is to imagine that the ball is resting at the narrow end of a funnel. (See Illustration #4.)

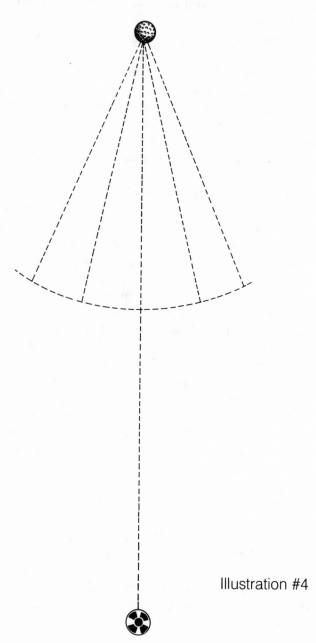

Illustration #4

The path of the ball is outward to somewhere on the outer edge of the funnel.

If you are a scatter-shot golfer, the funnel may extend clear across the fairway, from rough to rough, and occasionally even into out-of-bounds territory. The golfer with the slice will have a funnel that skews off to the right; the player with the hook tends to have a funnel that veers to the left.

Not every shot stays in the funnel; even a Nicklaus, Palmer, or Hogan occasionally belts one out of sight in the wrong direction. But generally, the better the golfer the narrower the funnel.

In 1982, for example, Calvin Peete ranked fourth among the money winners, and two statistics told why: He hit more than eighty-one percent of his drives onto the fairway—the best record on the tour, and he reached the green in regulation figures almost seventy-three percent of the time, which was also the best on the circuit.

By contrast, when I was on the tour I hit the fairway only half the time. Figuring that there are fourteen driving holes on the average course, Peete was in the fairway on eleven holes; I was on the fairway on only seven. If this were spread over a four-day tournament, he would be in the fairway sixteen more times than I would—a tremendous advantage.

I strongly recommend that you get in the habit of using your imagination and thinking of your long iron and wood shots in terms of a funnel. Make it a realistic funnel to accommodate most of your shots; not your "wish" shots, but the ones you normally hit.

Then, as you work on your game you can use the funnel as a guide, gradually reducing its width as your accuracy improves.

One detail in setting up your first drive often gets overlooked: The simple act of teeing up the ball.

Actually it isn't that simple. The ball should be teed up in such a position that when your club strikes it, it does so with the center of the clubface—the place professionals call the "sweet spot."

Some professionals will vary the height of the tee depending upon the club they're using; generally, the more lofted the clubface the closer to the ground they place the tee.

Others have a uniform height for their tee, in the belief that you basically swing all clubs in the same way regardless of the differences in the loft of the club.

My own style is to tee up so that the top of the driver is level with the middle of the golf ball. Whenever I use any other club, I tee it up as close to the ground as possible.

Every once in a while you see a high-handicap player teeing up high, apparently on the theory that it will help get the ball into the air. But that's not what makes the ball airborne. It is the loft of the club.

It is also important to know just why you tee up the ball. You tee up when you use the driver because you are hitting with a club that has only 9 or 10 degrees of loft. Since every other club has more loft, you don't need the tee. You want to use the tee solely to give you a good lie for your ball.

Contrary to what some amateurs believe, there is no advantage in shooting off the turf if you don't have to. Whether you are using a wood or an iron off the tee, you are much better off taking advantage of the perfect lie you have with a teed-up ball.

When using your irons for driving the only thing to remember is that you must still hit down through the ball and take turf afterward. Otherwise, your shots will have no backspin to "bite" the green.

The best way to judge whether your technique in teeing up the ball is the right one for your game is to observe what happens when you hit the ball. If it isn't behaving the way you want, check to see if the position of the tee is distorting the arc of your swing.

Once you've settled on a tee position, be consistent. Always tee up in the same way. The only reason to ever change is if you find new problems in your game, and you feel it necessary to re-evaluate your tee position. Even then, think twice. The more things you can do automatically in golf, the better your opportunity to concentrate on hitting the ball.

Frankly, I don't always follow that advice in my own game. For some reason or another, if I get more confident in my game I have a tendency to tee the ball a little higher, and if I am not driving all that well, I tee it a little lower. I've noticed that a number of other pros do the same thing. I don't really think it alters the game, but perhaps it helps psychologically.

As you've already noted, I don't put much stock in wishful thinking on the golf course, but I do put a lot of weight on positive thinking. So if you find a mannerism or a slight adjustment in your game that doesn't fit the "book" but gets results for you, be my guest!

We have been discussing a number of decisions you have to make. Many of them are leading up to the next question: Exactly where do you want your first shot to land?

First you must establish your "funnel"—the part of the course within which you expect your ball to land. You are the only one who can know that answer. It depends on your game, the distance you hit, and accuracy that you can normally expect.

This is no time for wishful thinking. You may like to think you are going to send a rocket down the middle of the fairway, but you have to ask yourself truthfully whether that is likely to be the way the ball actually flies.

Again, be conservative. Play "within" yourself.

You can begin by establishing the distance you think your drive will go. That doesn't mean the distance your better drives customarily travel. Be realistic and you'll find that it pays off in greater accuracy.

Next, look down the fairway to the spot where you think your ball will land, then fill in your imaginary "funnel." At this point you have a pretty good picture of what you're aiming for. You are no longer "shooting at the world."

Let's narrow it down a bit more. If you hit the ball where you'd like to, what will happen next? What kind of position will you be in for your next shot? Will it take you directly toward the green, or will you face a hazard that could give you trouble?

And what about the shot after that? Will it be a clear shot at

the green? Is your way the best pathway to the pin? (See Illustration #5.)

This is a good place to begin learning to project yourself from tee to green as you size up each hole. Plan ahead so that if all goes well you improve your percentages of success with each succeeding shot.

It is also a good time to take a fresh look at your "funnel." Ask yourself these questions:

- What are the risks and rewards if you use that target for your drive?
- How much trouble are you inviting if your shot goes to the left edge of the funnel? Or the right edge?
- Does most of the funnel cover an arc where you feel reasonably comfortable, or will you be better off shifting your target area to another location?

It is important to make these evaluations with the right combination of confidence and caution. You don't want to play timid golf; nor do you want to be reckless. You want to find the blend that works for you.

My own attitude is to respect trouble, but to try not to let it dominate my thinking. I plan on hitting good shots; if I don't, I'll tackle the consequences when I come to them.

That's not being cocky or reckless, it is being confident in my game. If you set realistic goals, you too ought to be able to count on your golf abilities. The doubter winds up with a timid and uninteresting approach to golf, and that's not for me. Nor, I suspect, for most of you.

Moreover, you can't hide from all the hazards. If there is water on both sides of the fairway, you've got to take a chance that you can keep the ball down the middle.

If you hit a "safe" shot with a short iron, for example, you may have more assurance of staying out of trouble, but only for that first shot. You will still have to go to a fairway wood for your second shot, and even then you will probably have taken away any percentage of getting down in par or even one-over.

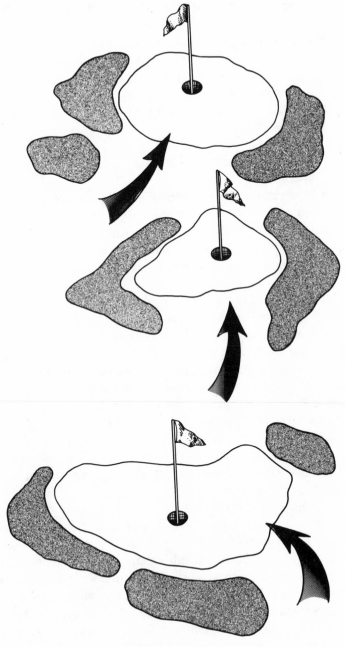

Illustration #5

It is a matter of risk and reward.

I can remember two cases in which caution paid off. In the first, Andy Bean was playing in the Doral Open. He had a two-stroke lead going into the eighteenth, and if he held on he would win his first tournament. It was a very tricky hole and Andy took a novel approach. He deliberately hit an iron off to the right, away from a water hazard; hit a second iron back toward the green; then hit a wedge onto the green and holed out with two putts.

It wasn't the way anybody else played that hole, but the bottom line was that it worked. Bean stayed out of trouble and won the tournament.

In the second case, Ray Floyd was playing the Kemper Open at Quail Hollow in Charlotte, North Carolina in 1975 and came to the seventy-second hole with a two-stroke lead. On the right, that final hole had a fairway bunker that was murder. Floyd knew that if he got into that bunker he could never get out to the green in one shot; as a matter of fact he could double-bogey if he slipped just a little, and that might be enough to cost him the tournament.

So he hit an iron off the tee to make sure his ball landed short of that treacherous bunker. He was then able to gamble with a 3-wood to the green because it was big enough to hold a wood shot, and even if the ball went into one of the traps that surrounded the green, Floyd was confident that he could get out of trouble and still have a safe two-putt hole out.

And that's the way he played it.

It is worth noting, however, that if his lead had been only one stroke, he probably could not have afforded to play safe. That would have left him vulnerable to one of the players just behind him, who could have picked up that one stroke and forced a playoff.

I suppose you could call what Andy Bean and Ray Floyd did "conservative" golf. But I think you could better call it "smart" golf. They figured out the odds in playing their situations in each of several different ways, and chose the one they believed gave them the best opportunity to win.

Chapter 4

Planning Your Golf Strategy

It is about ten in the morning on a bright Sunday in October, with clear skies and a wind, out of the south, of about fifteen miles an hour. Normally at this time of year most foursomes will waive the customary rules and permit a golfer to move his ball and tee it up on the fairway. But on this day there aren't a lot of leaves and the fairways are in good shape, so our foursome elects to play by regular summer rules.

As I walk to the tee, I try to take in the overall makeup of the hole. This is the time to put into practice the preparation we have already discussed in this book: the steps leading up to the first shot.

Too many players, even low-handicap players, don't have any kind of plan for their play. They only want to keep the ball in the fairway, which is a good rule but isn't enough.

Where in the fairway?

Where are you aiming each shot? And why?

Obviously, it makes a difference whether you hit the ball 150 yards or 250 yards. The 250-yard hitter can hope to reach some of the par-5 greens with two good shots; the shorter hitter will probably need three. The big hitter can ''reach'' the shorter par-5s with his drive and an iron; other golfers aren't going to match those shots.

But regardless of how far you hit the ball, the principles of

sound golf apply. You must know where you want the ball to go, why you want it to go there, and how big a margin of error you can expect on each shot.

That's the thought process you should go through. Then comes the execution, and if I were to define good golf performance simply, it would be the following: Hitting each shot so that the next one is easier. If your drive is well placed, your second shot is easier. If your second shot is an approach and it is well executed, you have an opportunity for a good chip shot. If your chip shot is stroked properly, you have a gimme putt.

As we know, not every shot turns out the way you planned it. But the basic concept remains unchanged. If your drive doesn't end up where you'd like it to, try to set up your second shot so that you have a chance for a decent third shot.

Let me give you a common example. Your drive winds up in the rough. If you follow the rule that each shot should make the next one easier, it is obvious that your first consideration is to get the ball out into the fairway, so that you at least have a decent lie for your follow-up.

If in addition to reaching the fairway you can put the ball in a good spot for your third shot, so much the better; but first give the highest priority to escaping the rough.

Let's pursue this concept further. Suppose your drive is good but your second shot goes off line. Your task now is to produce a third shot that makes your fourth one as potentially productive as possible. A good illustration of such a third shot would be a well-placed approach or chip shot that gives you the best odds for a successful putt.

And so it goes, with each shot aimed at making the next one easier. Keep this goal in mind as we go back to the golf course and I show you how I plan the one-shot-at-a-time approach, visualizing how it will affect the shot that follows.

I'll also show you how you have to constantly revise your thinking to adjust to where your ball actually goes, not where you had hoped it would go.

The first hole on Olympia Fields' north course is a very slight dogleg to the left. It is one of the longer holes on the

course, and it has an out-of-bounds area to the left and sand traps and bunkers guarding the right.

We already know that the first hole on any course is usually not terribly challenging from the standpoint of difficulty. It is like an alertness test: any drowsiness will show up immediately; if you are alert, you'll start making the right judgment calls.

The first fairway at Olympia Fields faces almost straight north, and the wind today will therefore give me a little more carry. The regular first-hole tee is 485 yards from the green, but our foursome chooses to play the championship 525 yard tee-to-green distance. (See Illustration #6.)

The par is 5.

There is something special about a par-5 hole. The professional golfer regards it as a possible birdie hole, a chance to pick up a stroke on par. An opening par-5 is especially inviting because it may be less demanding than the par-5s you encounter later in the round.

All strokes are important, but if you're going to succeed in knocking off a stroke on a par-5, the premium is on your second shot. Assuming a fairly decent drive, your second shot is the one which—when correctly done—puts you into a chip-and-one-putt situation.

Olympia Fields' first hole is pretty much open on the right; an extreme slice will put your ball into the adjacent ninth fairway.

When you find yourself in this situation, you should be aware of a very common mistake made on any hole on which there is a lot of open space on the right (or on the left): the tendency to overcompensate for danger in one place and wind up finding it in another.

That is true in this case. With all that real estate to shoot for, there is a tendency to go too far right. There are some bothersome trees bordering the fairway on the right, and if you land in that area you could find yourself blocked on your second shot.

Even if you avoid that problem, a long shot to the right adds unnecessary yardage to your shots to the green. The biggest

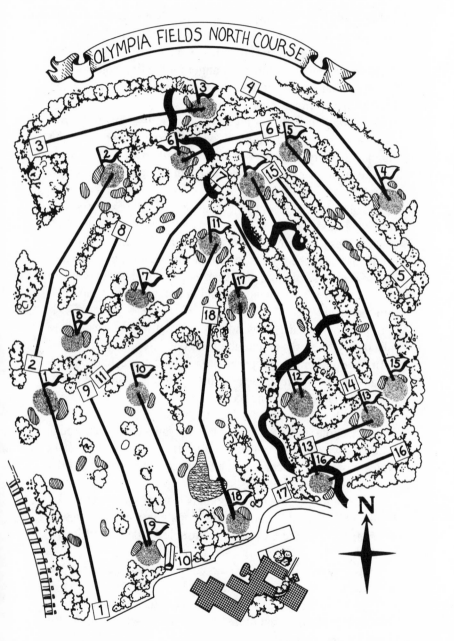

Illustration #6

problem of going too far right, however, is that you are in the wrong part of the fairway: your second shot will be headed straight for the trap in front of the green.

However, the real source of danger on the first hole isn't on the right, but on the left—an out-of-bounds area along the neighboring railroad track.

The good golfer always takes a second look at any hole with an out-of-bounds area. In many ways the out-of-bounds is the toughest penalty in golf. You not only suffer a penalty stroke but have to hit the ball a second time from as near to your original position as possible.

So I always treat an out-of-bounds with a little extra respect. And so should you.

This doesn't mean that you should fear any hazard. I find it ironic that many beginners, when they come up against a water hazard, are so afraid that they freeze up and like as not wind up doing exactly what they were afraid of doing: sending their ball into the drink.

On the other hand, it is not uncommon for the amateur to mistakenly be fairly casual about an out-of-bounds.

In my opinion, the proper approach is to evaluate each hazard as you come to it and seek, where you can, to nullify its potential for damaging your score.

That's the case here.

On this hole, there are a good twenty yards between the edge of the fairway and the out-of-bounds fence, so it really doesn't concern me very much. It will take an extreme hook or a badly hit ball to go out of bounds.

But even though the out-of-bounds is not a serious problem, I still follow the rule most professionals use in dealing with trouble: I tee up the ball on the "trouble" side. (See Illustration #7.)

Thus, my ball is on the left side of the driving area, my perspective is now away from the trouble.

This serves a double purpose. It lessens the chance of hitting into the trouble area, but more importantly, it sets me up for the route I want my ball to take.

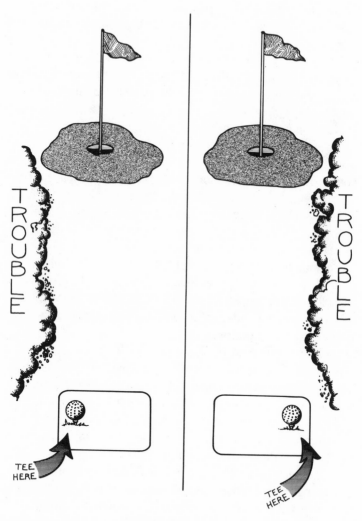

Illustration #7

I want to start the ball down the right hand side of the fairway and have it draw in toward the middle of the fairway. Teeing off from the left side gives me a slight advantage in doing that, and as I've said before, it pays to pick up an edge anywhere you can.

Our tentative plan now is for a drive that will go to the right so as to avoid any possibility of going into the out-of-bounds area on the left, but not so far right that we run into headaches farther on.

Next we have to think about our second shot.

One of the things you learn from experience is that trouble usually crops up in pairs. Only rarely is there a spot on the golf course in which you're facing only one trouble area. So from the tee, you look to see where the other trouble spots are.

Sure enough, there are two traps about a third of the way down the fairway. They are too close to bother our foursome, but farther on is another pair of traps.

The one on the left lies about 220 yards out. If I hit a really poor shot, it could be a problem. But a more likely danger is from the other trap, which is on the right, about 250 yards out. It lies right in the middle of my driving area and extends about five yards into the fairway.

Still farther on are two traps guarding the green. The one we should be concerned about is the one on the right. It extends almost halfway across the green. If we let that trap get between us and the cup, we will have to deal with it.

The simple answer is to avoid it, if we can, by going for the open space to the left, where there is no guard trap. That opening is the "gateway" to the green.

If I am playing well I'll hit the ball so that my approach travels through that corridor. Why? Because if I hit short for any reason, I will still have a straightaway shot to the pin; I won't be in the sand trap or have to take the chance of pitching over it.

In summary, our most effective strategy is to stay out of the trouble on the left with our drive, but return to the left-hand side of the fairway with our second shot so that we have the

easiest and clearest path to the cup, while at the same time avoiding the traps on the right.

Making this work will involve some tradeoffs. If we emphasize safety on our drive, we will aim out to the right, away from trouble. But the farther to the right we hit our drive, the farther away we are from the left-hand edge of the fairway, which is where we want to be when we get close to the green.

There is a workable compromise: aim to the right, shooting away from the troublesome out-of-bounds on the left, but don't overdo it. We want to give away as little of the left fairway as we can while still being safe.

If I can hit a well-placed drive, I will avoid the trap on the right, and most importantly will be set up for that key second shot. I will have a good shot straight for the green.

My specific goal is to put the ball out about 250 yards and within a 15-yard circle between the trap and the rough. To do that I aim the ball down the center of the fairway with a slight draw. This means that the ball will follow a fairly straight path but will curve slightly to the left at the end.

My swing feels comfortable and I make good contact with the ball. How do I know? I can tell because of the sound—it is not unlike the sound of hitting a baseball with a broken bat.

But instead of following the path I had planned, the ball starts going too far to the left. It hooks, but because of its poor start winds up about five yards into the left rough.

We can now see the advantage of taking precautions. Teeing off on the same side as the trouble area paid off. Had I teed off on the right, the ball could well have hooked into the out-of-bounds area.

What went wrong? I had the right strategy, my swing felt good, and the sound of my shot indicated I had hit the ball squarely.

There was an obvious reason why the ball didn't behave. I had broken one of the rules I spoke of earlier: Adequate preparation. I had only a brief warmup, three putts and two 7-iron shots. My swing was good but, as often happens when you

aren't warmed up, I didn't move my left side as well as I should have, and my direction was off.

Another factor might have contributed to the way the drive went. My woods were made in 1950 and I take extra good care of them. Today, however, I had my driver and 3-wood in the shop for refinishing.

Compared to my regular woods, my spare clubs are a little bit weaker. Normally the more flexible shaft makes you hit higher and hook a little bit more. Today my shot turned out not necessarily higher, but did hook more than usual.

Clubs are only one of many variables that affect the flight of the ball. The prime cause of erratic flight is inconsistency. If your swing is inconsistent, the results are going to be inconsistent. You can't really be sure where the ball is going to go.

But even if you are swinging well there are still many things that can happen. It is safe to say that there is no such thing as a perfect shot every time. Even the best golfers don't hit the ''sweet spot'' consistently.

Golf is a game of inches; driving isn't just a matter of inches, it is a matter of small fractions of an inch. Thus, even with a good setup and a smooth swing there are still at least three different shots you can hit.

You can catch the ball on the heel of the club, which indicates that your swing was only a shade off target. A ball hit in that fashion usually starts to the left, then goes to the right.

That's because you are slightly outside the correct plane of the swing when you make contact with the ball, and it takes your shot slightly to the right of your target.

The opposite is to swing too far inside the correct plane. In this case, even with a good swing, you hit the ball on the toe of the club and it starts out some ten to fifteen yards to the right of the target. Your clubface, at impact, is closed, resulting in a shot that hooks.

There are a few great drivers like Lee Trevino who consistently hit the ball in the fairway. But most of us have to live with our errors and adjust to them.

One penalty for not hitting the ball where you want it to go is

landing in the rough. And that is exactly what has happened to me on the first drive. There are times when you are as well or even better off in the rough than in the fairway, but they are few. Winning golfers are usually in the fairway.

The penalty I pay for landing in the rough is the loss of opportunity. Had I put the ball where I wanted, I might have had a shot at the green. The pin was ideally located—deep in the green—so there was enough room for the ball to roll. Depending on my lie, I would have had a chance to shoot for the green or, if necessary, lay the ball up just short of the green, with enough resistance from the fringe grass to stop it.

That was the difference. From a fairway lie, I could have concentrated on my position on the green; from the rough, I've got to focus my attention to getting the ball out of trouble.

The first thing to do in this case is dismiss the drive from my mind. As I've already said, it isn't going to do any good to worry now about the shot I didn't make. That's behind me. What I've got to do is concentrate on my second shot.

Even though my drive didn't land where I had hoped, the basic rule still applies. Each shot must be planned to make the next one easier. Now my task is to adjust to the new challenge and put the ball where it will be in the best possible location for my third shot.

It won't be hard to get out of the rough. It is less grown up now, in the fall, than it was earlier in the year. The grass is dormant and probably two inches high instead of three or four. It isn't going to give me much trouble; still, it will give me enough.

Let me explain what I mean by trouble.

Where I will have difficulty is with control. When you hit a ball out of the rough, it has very little spin. Its trajectory is higher, and you can't be confident either of distance or of the amount of roll the ball will have after landing. Moreover, at this time of year the greens are firmer and it is harder to control your approach shots.

Here, then, is the picture: Because my drive landed in the

rough, my plans for my second shot must change. I can no longer go for the green without taking a needless gamble.

However, because I can see that the pin is in the rear of the green, my strategy will now be to lay the ball up short of the green and in line with the left gateway to the hole.

From that position I will have the whole green to pitch to, and can get close enough for an easy par or even a birdie four; a great way to start.

I pick the right club—the 3-wood will carry me to the green but not overshoot it.

In my opinion, overshooting the green is one of the worst errors in golf. It can be a disaster for a number of reasons.

One, the rough in back of the green is usually more overgrown and rugged than in most other places on the course.

Two, you have a shot with a low percentage of success. You are likely to have a rough time just getting the ball on the green, let alone in any sort of decent position.

Worse, you are almost always forced to pitch onto a downward sloping green surface, which is one of the tougher shots in the game.

As a result, when you go over the green you have usually lost any opportunity for a birdie; getting a par is difficult; and there is the threat of a bogie and worse.

For all of these reasons I strongly recommend backing down one club if there is a danger of overshooting the green. In this case, that means I should choose a 3-wood.

I make a good contact with the ball but encounter the difficulty I mentioned earlier. Out of the rough a ball tends to fly without spin and it isn't totally controllable.

This particular shot has both poor direction and more roll than I wanted. Specifically, the ball lands too far right and keeps on rolling into the right bunker.

It certainly wasn't the shot I wanted. If it had gone as I had planned, the ball would have wound up about fifteen yards to the left of the bunker, where I would have had the whole green to shoot at. But given the problems of shooting from the rough

with a fairway wood, the shot came within a reasonable margin of error.

That evaluation would not apply to a higher handicap player. To land in a trap could be a more serious error for a weekend golfer because he is usually unsure of himself in a bunker.

A pro, however, normally finds trap shots easier to control than those out of the rough, unless the ball is buried, and in this case mine is not. Besides, there are some favorable circumstances of my lie; because the pin is deep, about thirty yards from the bunker, I have a lot of green to work with.

One thing you find as you study golf carefully is the importance of pin placement. More than anything else it dictates your approach and chip shots. Ideally you always want to hit into the biggest part of the green, and that will depend on where the hole is cut.

This is another situation in which the pro has an advantage over the amateur.

When you play in a pro tournament, the pin positions are changed daily. At tee-off time you are given a chart showing the placement of the pins for that day. That information, combined with the yardage book, gives you a blueprint for your approach.

When you are on the tee in regular play, however, you have only a general impression of where the hole is. You don't know exactly what you are going to find on the green, and you probably won't know until you get to your approach shot. But at that point, if you are going to play intelligently you *must* know.

To review my situation, even though my ball is in a sand trap, I am not too concerned. I have confidence that I have the right line to the cup; that comes from experience. What is more difficult is judging distance.

Late in the season the traps aren't raked often and they become crusty. The ball comes out faster and without much spin. Without spin, you lose a measure of control over the ball. And that's what happens to me.

I hit a sand wedge and carry the ball a little too far to be in perfect position. In July the ball would have stopped more

quickly; as it was it went about four feet past the pin, leaving me a downhill, four-foot putt.

I would have been better off short; downhill putts are more difficult than uphill ones. But at this point I get a break. Two of the other players have the same putt, but longer.

Since they have to putt first, I have a chance to watch how their ball reacts to the green, and it is clear that its roll is almost straight, with only a fraction of a left-to-right break. It is a putt you want to aim toward the left center of the hole, and I can it for my birdie.

Let's analyze what has happened.

Going back over the hole, only one shot—the putt—followed exactly what I wanted it to do. My drive was off line to the left; my fairway approach carried too far right; and my sand shot went too long.

Put that way, it was a poor showing; only one in four shots went according to plan. But my birdie was not a ''fluke''; it was actually a fairly well-played hole. And here's why:

Even though three of my shots weren't perfect, we've already agreed that nobody plays perfect golf. The key to scoring well in golf usually isn't how good your good shots are, but how good your bad shots are.

If you consider my first three shots ''bad''—and they sure weren't what I wanted—they were pretty good ''bad'' shots. None of them got me in serious trouble and none cost me a stroke.

Even if they weren't executed as well as I had hoped, they were planned in such a way as to minimize the damage they did. Thus, while my problems began with an off-line drive, I was later able to make up for it with a good escape from the trap and a sound putt.

By contrast, the other golfers in our foursome made errors but couldn't recover.

For example, one of them started out better than I did. He outdrove me by about fifteen yards, but failed on the crucial

second shot. He left his ball in the right rough—the one place on this hole where a golfer doesn't want to be.

It forced him to shoot over the trap and then attempt to stop his ball in time for a decent putt. Not surprisingly, he was unable to bring off this very difficult shot.

My partner also had one bad shot. He drove into the rough, but then he correctly recovered back onto the fairway. When you drive into the rough on a par-5 hole, the most important thing is to get your second shot close to the green—but above all on the fairway.

Instead, my partner then made a very bad shot. He misjudged his approach. He had plenty of green to shoot for and only a seventy-yard carry, but he ended up in the trap. He exploded well and putted for a par.

You have just come along with our foursome as we played the first hole at Olympia Fields. You've seen each of us make at least one mistake, and have been able to assess the damage it caused.

Now the question is: How can you translate these shots into your own game?

First, you have to know your capabilities off the tee. Had you been part of our foursome, and if your drives are normally about 175 yards long, you would have had to play the hole differently than we did. For example, you could not have expected to reach the green in two shots.

More likely, it would take three good shots to put you on or near the green. Nor, short of a super-approach or chip shot, would it have been easy for you to birdie this hole. Even par is not going to be easy for the 100-plus player.

The hole will "play" differently for the shorter hitter. There is an extra set of fairway traps on the first hole. They didn't concern our foursome because they were only about 175 yards out. Our drives cleared that area easily, but for many golfers this is about where their ball will land.

If that is your case, winning strategy calls for a shot down the center of the fairway and, if need be, just short of the traps.

For the shorter hitter, the next two shots should be in the fairway and on the left, so that the ball winds up, as it does with the pro, in the gateway entrance to the green.

What if your drives go just over 200 yards? In that case you will easily carry the first set of traps, but the next trap on the left is about 220 yards out and you should assess its potential for trouble.

If your drives don't normally carry that far, you can even use that trap as a target, because doing so will keep your ball on the left side of the fairway, which is eventually where you want to wind up.

If the trap constitutes a threat, however, I recommend aiming to the right, away from it, but with as limited a safety factor as you can afford, because your second shot should be directed toward that left-hand-side opening to the green.

The third shot for most golfers will be the key to their score. There will be a temptation to go for the green, and if you have put together two good shots you may be in a good position to try for it.

The best way to decide what to do is to stop and check out the theory of risk-reward. If you can reach the green, how much better off will you be? What is the penalty if you fail to reach the green? If you don't, where will the ball wind up?

If the ball winds up over the green you're in bogey country. If it lands short, but to the right, you have lost your opening to the green and your fourth shot will have to go over the guarding trap, which can also spell trouble.

What you may find is that your most profitable course is to lay the ball up short of the green with your third shot and then rely on a chip and a putt to achieve a par. Depending on your game, that can be a good score; regardless of your game, par is a lot better than bogey or double-bogey.

Think about it.

One thing stands out. What the weekender should avoid, if at all possible, is getting into the rough where he will lose both distance and control. A 175-yard drive and two properly placed fairway shots of 160 yards each and you're near the green in

regulation figures. An off-line shot or a ball in the rough or a trap, and your chance for a par goes down considerably.

The pros have a phrase for it: Keep the ball in play.

That means out of trouble and on the fairway.

But if you don't, be sure to get your next shot back on the fairway; don't give yourself any unnecessary shots.

Then get on the green and down in two, and you're on your way to lower scores and more enjoyment on the links.

Chapter 5

Developing Golf Imagination

Before we go to the second tee and continue our round at Olympia Fields, I'd like to talk a little more about golf imagination. I don't think any golfer really starts learning the game until he develops such imagination.

What do I mean by golf imagination? I mean an ability to "see" in your mind what happens to a golf ball when you hit it. How far it goes. The path it takes. How far it rolls. What happens when you hit a golf ball correctly and what happens when you make an error.

But golf imagination is more than just visualizing the flight of the ball. It is applying that knowledge to meet the challenge of the golf shot you attempt. It is planning ahead to decide which club is best suited to the shot you're attempting. It is evaluating in your mind where the ball will go if you are successful and where it may go if you are not.

How do you develop a golf imagination?

First you must understand that the game of golf never changes. You swing at a golf ball in the same way whether you're playing in Chicago, Tokyo, London or Hometown U.S.A.

What does change are the golf courses. Because no two are alike, it isn't enough to understand the shots I used on the first hole at Olympia Fields; you must understand why I used them.

You must be able to imagine just what approach you would take if you were playing that same hole. That ability is what I call golf imagination.

Let me illustrate what I mean, using the first hole.

There were three challenges: the out-of-bounds left, the trees on the right and the bunker that guarded the green. The intelligent golfer must not only recognize the existence of these hazards, but understand what the architect had in mind. Why he chose each particular hazard, why he located it where he did and what he is challenging you to do.

Earlier we discussed how futile it is to "shoot at the world" if you are going to improve your game.

It is equally difficult to progress in learning the game until you grasp the concept of just why each golf hole represents a new and different challenge, and more importantly, what to do about it.

Each hazard on a well-designed golf course has a reason: to make the course more interesting. Golf would be a much simpler game—but neither as challenging or as much fun—if every shot wound up in a level place in the fairway or straightaway to the hole.

Water, sand, trees, out-of-bounds areas, and other hazards are important to the game. Without them, golf would be just a matter of hitting the ball until you reached the green and then the cup. There would be little strategy except to hit the ball as far as possible, and any golfer could get by with a couple of woods, a short iron, and a putter.

But that's not the way golf is, even on those public courses designed more for speed of play than quality golf.

Every course has its own unique design and requires you to use most, if not all, of your clubs. It rewards you for a properly selected and executed shot and makes you pay a penalty for one that isn't.

That's where golf imagination comes in. Golfers who finish high in the money in any given tournament are those who have a good golf imagination. They not only know how to execute

the shots, they know the right ones to use for most effectively challenging the course.

But probably those who have the best golf imagination of all are the golf architects. Small wonder, then, that Jack Nicklaus and some of the other top golfers have designed their own courses.

I have played hundreds of courses over the years. Each was different from the others in some particulars, but nearly all carried the imprint of the man who designed it. It seems logical, then, that one way to learn how to properly play a course is to understand the thinking behind its creation.

With that thought in mind, let's visit two nationally known golf architects, Lawrence and Roger Packard of LaGrange, Illinois, and see if we can pick up some pointers.

Among the courses the Packard firm has designed are the Innisbrook complex—the Copperhead, Sandpiper, and Island courses at Tarpon Springs, Florida—and the Ladies Professional Golf Association course, Sweetwater, in Houston, Texas.

Just as no two golf courses are alike, neither are the styles of golf architects alike. Pete Dye makes imaginative use of railroad ties in his designs. In some of their more recent designs, George and Tom Fazio have used contouring, creating level areas on the fairway for which the player can aim. The Joneses (Robert Trent and sons Reese and Robert Trent, Jr.) repeat some of their favorite designs, which helps the knowledgeable player spot one of their courses.

Knowing the architects' styles is a plus, particularly when you are playing a layout for the first time. Sometimes, such familiarity can help you anticipate trouble ahead on the hole. Experience playing on one course sometimes gives you a hint how to play another designed by the same architect.

There are many levels of golf courses. They range from short, so-called pitch-and-putt layouts to the name courses you see on television. The design of each course varies widely, depending in part on its purpose.

The Packard firm has designed some of those tournament

layouts, but most of their effort is aimed at the amateur. Those which the Packards have designed for the pro differ in many ways from those planned for the amateur, but the major contrast is in the length.

That factor alone—length—separates many golf courses in terms of difficulty. According to Larry Packard, the longer the course, the more strokes the player is going to take, and he believes that this holds true for pro and hacker alike.

If so, when you are a visiting player at a course where you've never golfed before, take a look at the total distance listed on the scorecard and adjust your handicap accordingly.

I don't agree totally with Larry about distance. It is a factor in judging the difficulty of a course, particularly for short-hitting amateurs; and it is logical that if you take two similar courses, the longer one will be the more difficult. But to better players, other factors than length are important.

I happen to think, for example, that trees are a major item in assessing the difficulty of a golf course. I played the course at Purdue University regularly during the four years I attended school there. Then, many years later, I went back for the first time since my graduation, and couldn't get over how much more difficult the course had become, simply because the trees had grown, changing the character of the course markedly.

Gary Groh tells the same story. He got to Medinah Country Club late Wednesday afternoon, just before the 1975 National Open. He and Sam Snead got to the thirteenth hole just as it was starting to get too dark to play. This is one of the most difficult on the course: a par-4, about a 460-yard dogleg left.

Groh asked Sam where he should hit his drive, and Sam recommended taking a shortcut by hitting the ball over the trees at the corner of the dogleg. The ball hit up into the trees and dribbled down. From there Groh had to scramble to get a bogey 5.

"Sam," he said indignantly, "what made you give me that advice?"

"Well," replied Sam, "that's the way I played it in the last tournament here."

That "last tournament," it turned out, had taken place in

91

1949, some twenty-six years earlier, and with the passing years the trees had grown a lot taller and fuller.

The trees at Medinah are one of its notable characteristics, but not the sole reason for its greatness. The latter comes from a combination of many factors. But probably the most significant test of Medinah or any other golf course is the quality of the players who use it.

Incidentally, it was the Packards that Medinah chose when it decided to revamp several holes on the back 9 to accommodate the Senior Tournament in 1989 and the U.S. Open in 1990.

Major tournaments are held at "name" courses designed to challenge golfers capable of playing par golf or better. Usually, however, a golf course must be able to cater to a wide variety of talent.

The membership at most clubs is rarely uniform. Duffers and low handicappers play the same course. Some compromising by the architect is essential if he is to meet the needs of the club.

Larry Packard explains this by pointing out that "The good players don't like any hole where they have to hold back. They resent a layup shot. They like to be able to slam out everything. I don't necessarily agree with their point of view, but wherever possible, we try to allow for full tee shots.

"In addition, you try to take care of the women golfers and the average man," says Packard. "You want to design the holes so these players are not in trouble constantly, but at the same time provide some of the hazards for the low-handicap players so they really have to think about their game.

"You try to create strategy dilemmas. For example, can they carry that bunker or water? This becomes a question of their golfing ability, and they must answer before they proceed. If they have doubts, what are their alternatives?

"On the other hand, if they can hit the ball hard and be twenty yards farther out, fine. But it means they have to hit a really good shot. Those are the challenges we try to present on every hole."

Creating a plan for a golf course isn't simply a matter of

scooping out dirt and rearranging the landscape. Many of today's golf courses are being designed around housing developments and shopping centers, and each layout has to fit together like a jigsaw puzzle.

Moreover, the basics of a golf course involve a complicated engineering plan. Planning the course requires explicit knowledge of the terrain, the surroundings, and the land limitations, plus a sharp pencil for keeping costs in line.

Among other details the architect must consider are the plans for watering the course and providing for drainage, pathways for golf carts, provisions for structures on the course, and concepts for its maintenance. And these are just a few of the details.

Those "housekeeping" details play a significant part in how well a golf course plays, for example, even though you and I usually pay little attention to them. Instead, most of our concern centers on how the golf architect has planned each hole, and in particular, the problems he has created for us.

Roger Packard puts it this way, "When you play a golf course, you should be looking at the areas the architect has given you, the places you are required to hit to and, depending on your game, which of them give you advantages and which give you disadvantages."

That's what I meant earlier when I talked about "risk-reward."

Roger provides one hint I think you will find helpful. Unless they have been modernized in recent years, older golf courses tend to play short. They were designed before today's improved clubs and balls, and are geared to shorter drives.

On the other hand, if you're playing a modern course, it is likely to demand that you hit your drives about 200 yards. However, the modern layouts usually give the golfer a good target to shoot for.

If you are an average golfer, you can aim down the middle of the fairway and be likely to have at least twenty yards of fairway on either side—plenty of real estate to accommodate hooks and slices.

On the other hand, the golfer who hits longer will have a greater challenge. He will have to improve his accuracy, because the fairways get progressively narrower as you pass the landing zone of the 200-yard hitter.

What about the golfer who can't hit 200 yards? He will have to adjust to a modern course. The "macho" golfer won't like this advice, but one way to make up for shorter drives is to switch to the forward tees.

I believe Roger Packard is right when he says that the old term "women's tees" may gradually be phased out for the more accurate description of "forward" tees.

These tees are set ahead of the regular tees and are designed to fit the game of juniors, women, and senior golfers who cannot challenge the more established golfer for distance off the tee, nor should they be required to.

There is a third set of tees—the championship tees—and their purpose is to provide an additional challenge to the better golfer by lengthening the distance of his tee shot. In theory, the choice of three tee positions "evens out" the course by accommodating the long ball hitter, the average golfer, and the short hitter.

I know that men who let their ego run their golf game will resist the idea of using forward tees but in my opinion, using the right tee makes sense.

The golfer who tries to hit farther than he really can is never going to improve his game, and will doom himself to unnecessary frustration when he should be enjoying the game.

Even if it meets resistance, I believe the forward-tee concept will gain increasing support, particularly from women golfers. Not only do they no longer accept second-class status on a golf course, welcoming the rethinking of tee placements, but they now have the numbers—there may be more women golfers today than men—and the power to force changes in golfing practice.

Roger Packard has another "inside" suggestion to help your golf planning. Older courses—those designed through the mid-

1970s—tend to have flat fairways. About the only exceptions are those on which the natural topography produced hills, valleys, and sidehill conformations.

That's not necessarily true any more. Many of the newer courses have added a new dimension to the fairways; besides bunkers, trees, and water, they have hitting areas designed into the fairways.

These "hitting areas" are usually high and level. They are meant to give the golfer special advantages—usually a better lie and better visibility for his next shot—if he can place the ball in that area.

By contrast, the golfer who fails to reach these locations may face uneven terrain and high ground obscuring his view for his next shot.

Regardless of their age, nearly all courses have one common ingredient: They have more trouble on the right than on the left. This is because the average golfer is more likely to slice his ball to the right than to hook it to the left.

If you want to think kindly about the golf architect, you can take the position that he wants to help you cure that problem, and so provides incentives in the form of traps and other hazards.

If you want to take a negative view, you can think he loads up the right-hand side simply to add more problems. In either case, if you are in doubt about the location and extent of the hazards, stay left. The odds are that you'll be safer there.

Whether the architect is influenced to create more trouble on the right or not, he does take human nature into account in many ways when laying out a golf course.

Earlier, we emphasized that it is a good idea for the golfer to warm up before he plays. But golf architects are realists. They know that most golfers aren't going to take the time to do this. So they frequently "soften up" the hazards on the first hole, and sometimes the second. That gives the lazy golfer time to warm up.

But don't get in the habit of using that excuse. Regardless of the difficulty, the first holes always play better if you come

prepared. Moreover, if the architect is charitable at the start of a round, he invariably makes up for it later.

Like most designers, the Packards try to make a special effort on the closing seventeenth and eighteenth holes. Again this involves human nature. Those final holes are a special challenge. If the golfer plays them well, it makes him feel good; if he fails, it gives him special motivation to come back for another try.

It is no coincidence that the final holes are the ones that are televised during major tournaments. There is, of course, the element of drama. But from a strictly golfing viewpoint, the closing holes on a well-designed course are intended to be the most difficult.

Typically, the hazards are tougher and more precision is required than on the opening holes. The golf architect makes a specific attempt to force the golfer to use strategy; to compel him to figure his own capabilities in handling the shots needed to close out the round.

The lesson is a clear one: Don't let down in the closing holes. If anything, be sharper mentally, and alert to the challenges built into those final holes.

As I've noted, most golf architects have specific guidelines that characterize the course they design. In the case of the Packards, no two holes on their golf courses are the same length.

They do this because they want you to employ all fourteen clubs in your bag. They believe that the true test of a golfer is an ability to handle a wide variety of challenges.

The Packards also believe in being "fair." They try to avoid any "blind" holes, so that your objective is always in sight.

"The old Scottish courses have a considerable number of pot bunkers that are hidden," explains Larry Packard. "You can hit a ball out there and you can roll into one if you are not familiar with the course. We think that's a little unfair. We don't know how a player can avoid a hazard if he can't see it."

The Packards try to make their water hazards "visible" too. But this is not always possible; for reasons of cost, there has to

be the occasional "hidden" problem. But an effort is made to avoid it.

In planning their courses, the Packards try to make the golfer feel "comfortable." One way to do this is to make it clear to the golfer just what the challenge is.

For example, on straightaway holes, they try to make it obvious from the tee just where the line is that separates the fairway from the hazards, so that the golfer won't be misled into trouble.

Doglegs pose a different problem for architect and golfer alike.

The golfer playing a course for the first time doesn't have an easy time knowing where to hit on a dogleg. The last half of the hole is hidden beyond the bend in the fairway. Lacking familiarity with the course, the visitor is forced to shoot blindly.

But if you are alert, you will find that the architect has offered the golfer some help: a general target area. This is the fairway area just beyond the bend—the place where drives will land if hit the proper distance.

A good rule of thumb in playing a strange course is to aim as close to the "bend" in the dogleg as you safely can. The better golfer will be able to "shave" the corner more closely and shorten the distance required on his next shot.

Once the golfer gets the ball inside that landing zone, he will have a clear view to the green.

Because not everybody is capable of pinpoint accuracy, the landing area is made large enough to take care of shots that wander off line. On the longer holes which require a second fairway shot, the landing area for the long woods and irons is also enlarged.

Here's a tip for playing dogleg holes: Look for the place where the fairway "balloons" out. That "extra" landing area is usually part of the "road map" to the green, and if you use it as a landmark it will give you a good idea of the right way to play the hole.

Let's take a look at the special challenges of the par-3 holes.

There are usually four par-3s on any course and they differ from the longer holes in one fundamental.

"On the par-4s and par-5s, you concentrate on the placement of your fairway shots," explains Larry Packard. "With the par-3s there is only one objective, and that is to get on the green with your tee shot."

A course designed by the Packards will follow one of their basic tenets—variety—of which distance is a component.

"Not every golf architect does this, but we make it a standard practice to have approximately twenty yards difference on each of the par-3s," says Packard. "This requires the golfer to use a different club off each of the tees."

The tee-to-flag distance is another variable. Today's greens are usually large enough to let the ground superintendent pick six different locations for the cup. Some courses are even equipped to vary the tees while at the same time keeping the distances to the greens unchanged.

Others, however, are limited to the three tee locations of forward, regular, and championship. As a result, the tee-to-green distances can vary as much as twenty yards on any given day.

"The smart golfer will pay attention to where the cup is cut and where the tee markers are," Packard points out.

Another tipoff: Shorter par-3 holes have tougher hazards and more difficult greens.

The Packards try to "size" their greens to match the approach shot—the longer the incoming shot, the larger the green. The same standards apply to their placement of traps. The more distance the approach shot has to cover, the wider the opening to the green.

You can use this knowledge to your advantage.

For example, one of the more difficult shots for the average golfer is a 3-wood shot with enough backspin to hold the green. If, as the Packards do, the architect provides a wide entranceway, you have the better option of hitting up short and letting the ball roll on.

The golf architect can also influence your game by the kind of green he specifies. Northern courses are based on bent

grass, which produces fast greens. It also makes the fairway rough difficult to play because the grass tends to get between the club and the ball.

By contrast, many southern courses are seeded with Bermuda grass. This is a grass that doesn't mat and it is harder to play from the rough. The most noticeable difference, however, is that Bermuda greens are much slower than those with a bent grass surface.

The distinction between the two kinds of playing surfaces is gradually blurring, however. There are some new strains of Bermuda grass that are moving steadily toward having the same characteristics as Northern bent. If you play Florida or Texas courses you might check that out.

In addition to "playability," about which we've talked a lot, there are many other considerations given to a golf course. The Packards put a heavy emphasis on beauty. Besides providing the golfer with a challenging round, they believe he should have pleasant surroundings.

They make a special effort to see that their courses blend into the landscape. Even the tees are fitted into the contours and irregular in shape, instead of being the traditional rectangles. Each green is of a different shape and size. And the traps designed by the Packards, while having a major role in the difficulty of a course, are large and scenic in nature.

A golf architect tries to take advantage of natural hazards such as rivers, ponds, or small lakes. As he plans the entire eighteen hole layout, he will often try to use water as a hazard on the shortest par-3 hole. Or, because it usually presents a very demanding tee shot, he may "save" it for one of the closing holes.

The architect may even further toughen up any hole by adding traps to snare shots that go off line. And as a final touch, if he feels the approach shot isn't challenging enough, he may put the green on a diagonal, which makes it narrower from front-to-back and requires greater accuracy off the tee.

As we have already pointed out, the smart golfer studies

each of these problems from the tee before he decides on his strategy.

One of the things the observant golfer will note is that there is often an alternative route to the cup. For example, the architect may provide a pathway to the green along one or the other side of the fairway.

One of these will be the challenging route, the other, normally extending a little short of the green, will present a "safer" way to the hole. The "bad news" is that it usually costs a stroke to take the safe way.

But even then the person playing the safe route can make up that stroke and still get a par by hitting a precision second shot stiff to the pin. The option to "go for it," play safe, or bank on a good chip shot is up to the golfer. The option you choose depends on your confidence in your game.

An example of the two-approach concept exists on one of the courses designed by the Packard firm—Eagle Ridge, near Galena, Illinois. In their preliminary design, the tenth hole presented them with a special problem.

There was a cliff that was an ideal location for the eleventh tee. But in order to use that site, they had to make the preceding tenth hole a shorter par-4 than they would have liked.

So they designed a hole for the adventurous and the cautious golfer alike. Between the tee and green is a knoll. In their design, the Packards covered it with a nest of traps to catch the golfer who tried, but failed, to get a solid hit. If he reached the green, he was rewarded, but if he hit short he was in trouble.

For the less confident golfer, they created a 150-foot fairway to the right, away from trouble. It provided ample space for any except the wildest-shooting golfer.

As a final touch of trouble, the Packards had to break their rule about "hidden" targets. The tenth hole at Eagle Ridge is one instance in which the golfer can't see the green until he reaches his second shot. It's hidden in back of the trap-covered knoll.

By now it is clear that there are no set rules for a golf archi-

tect, but that he is always seeking to ''even up'' the course if he can. If the distance between the tee and green is not particularly challenging, the architect will pay particular attention to ways of toughening it up.

For this same reason you can almost always anticipate problems when you get to a short par-5 hole. On such holes the golfer is likely to find more heavily guarded and tricky greens, and the reason for this is distance.

For the good or medium golfer, distance on a short par-5 is a snap. Take a 490-yard hole. A relatively short hitter can put together a drive and a 3-wood shot and be within 130 yards of the hole.

Under these circumstances the golfer's third shot may be even a shorter distance from the green than he would encounter on the shortest par-3. Longer hitters would have an even easier third shot; they would probably be no more than ten to fifteen feet off the green.

In terms of distance, then, the short par-5s are the easiest for a golfer to birdie. In order to prevent them from being too easy, the architect will reach into his bag of hazards.

One thing he may do is make the hole a dogleg with a water hazard, to require a more accurate drive. Or he may insert yet a second dogleg to compel the average golfer to play to the left or right of the green in order to play it safe.

But his design will still permit the more confident player to reach the green if he can get over the water or trap that intervenes. It provides a shot the good golfer can make, but forces him to work for his birdie.

Nor is it impossible for the average player to also get a birdie if he prefers to take the safe route, except then he must hit a good pitch or wedge shot to the flag.

But while par-5 holes usually provide an opportunity for the golfer to pick up strokes by using a smart strategy, they are also the places to take chances. And taking chances is one of Roger Packard's pet ideas.

Roger believes that the average golfer can find greater en-

joyment in the game if he occasionally tries a few bold shots.

"Nine times of out of ten it won't work," he says, "but it helps build confidence. Besides, it's fun to take a chance every once in a while."

I agree, at least to an extent. I feel that the golfer who gets too conservative limits his growth; he is taking some of the challenge out of the game. But I also believe that every golfer must first learn to put his ego in check and learn his capabilities and limitations before taking risks. And that's a hard lesson to learn.

Actually, if you want to take an occasional gamble, I think you should check out the par-4s on your course rather than the par-5s. Many of them are designed with a two-way approach— bold and conservative.

Par-4s usually run from 251 to 470 yards long, and they give the designer a lot of latitude. A par-4 hole can contain uphill, downhill, or sidehill fairways, doglegs or bends, fairway bunkers, water or trees—in fact, just about anything to provide a test of the golfer's skill.

Yet regardless of the kind and number of the hazards it holds, the par-4 hole will always have a preferred place for the average golfer to aim at so that he won't be in trouble and will have a fair opening to the green on his approach shot.

On a course designed by the Packards, the par-4s will generally have a forty-yard-wide target area, whose location will be be based on the assumption that the average player's tee shot will land somewhere between 180 and 240 yards out from the tee.

What about the professional golfer or long-hitting amateur? They really don't get that much "friendly" attention, at least on the average golf course. They make up such a small percentage of the golfing population that they aren't figured into most designs.

What the longer hitter does have to face is being better in terms of accuracy on the par-4 and par-5 holes. The fair-

ways are made narrower beyond the normal driving distances in an effort to require the long-ball hitter to be more precise.

As Larry Packard puts it, "If they are able to hit the ball 240 or 250 yards out, they ought to be able to place it a little better."

To make it even more demanding for the long-ball hitter, Packard often designs fairway traps at the bends in the doglegs. These bunkers are far enough out from the tee that they don't concern the shorter hitter, while giving the big hitter something to worry about.

"The high-handicap player is going to lose a stroke at the bend and a stroke at the green because he's going to be short all the time," Packard points out. "Why put a trap where he'll lose still another stroke?"

When designing dogleg holes, the Packard firm has another trademark that isn't shared by all golf-course architectural firms: They always provide plenty of open space beyond the bend so that there is plenty of fairway for any golfer's ball to land without winding up in the deep rough.

Larry thinks it is "unfair" to penalize a player for driving too far. As a result, the fairways on his courses provide ample room for long-distance drives.

Another point about which Packard feels strongly is a sand trap that doesn't trap anybody. In recent years many courses have "flattened" their bunkers so that the lip of the trap isn't a problem.

"Only now are some of the more sophisticated golf chairmen and operators realizing that it is senseless to spend money on a hazard if you can hit a ball almost as far out of it as you can if you weren't in it," says Packard, pointing out that in such a case "it loses all its value."

Packard illustrates this with one hole on a midwestern golf course that his firm is redesigning. Currently, if you land in the flat part of the bunker, you can actually hit the ball farther than if you were in the rough.

The Packards have also sought to eliminate traps in useless

locations. Women golfers complain—and justifiably—about traps located in the fairway at distances that penalize even a good drive by a woman. Many of these traps are ones left over from the days when women golfers were tolerated rather than welcomed, by the private clubs.

I have already discussed trees, but one of their functions that most golfers wouldn't be likely to note is safety. In making sure an errant shot doesn't jeopardize other players, the architect utilizes the distances between fairways and the spaces between the greens and the following tees.

In many instances, however, these distances by themselves are inadequate for safety. One answer to this is to plant trees to provide a ''shield.'' Besides blocking many shots, they also influence the golfer to avoid shots into the danger area.

Trees are also among the toughest hazards on a course. If you get behind a tree you lose your line of direction; if you get into a clump of trees you may have trouble finding a safe way out to the fairway.

Trees also bring a measure of luck into play. Two persons may hit the ball to spots only five yards apart, but one will land in the open and the other will be unlucky enough to land behind a tree.

''That's luck,'' says Larry Packard ''and to the extent that you reduce the element of luck, you make the course more fair. But there are those who contend that luck does—and should— play a part in golf.''

I remember Jack Nicklaus commenting that ''Golf wasn't intended to be fair.'' He was suggesting, I think, that part of the challenge of the game is to overcome the bad breaks we all run into on the golf course.

On a course that has knolls and swales, for example, one golfer may land on the flat part and another on a more difficult side-hill lie—a pure chance result.

But luck or no luck, the thinking-man's golfer usually evens up those breaks. Larry Packard puts his basic philosophy this way:

"What we emphasize is that you have to think on every shot. Where are you trying to go? We try to develop the placement concept; that there is a place for you to hit the ball on every shot in order to make the next shot a good one. If you can achieve that you'll play our courses very well."

That's good advice for playing any course.

After a bit we'll talk with two of the nation's best grounds-keepers and get some inside hints from them. But for the moment, it's time to put the advice of the Packards to work. So let's move to the second tee.

Chapter 6

Tackling the Doglegs

There are long holes and short holes in golf—and there are crooked holes. The crooked holes are doglegs where the fairway starts out straight but then turns to the left or right. Dogleg holes present special challenges because, in contrast to straightaways, they are less tolerant of shots that hook or slice markedly.

I enjoy playing the doglegs. They make the game more interesting. It takes imagination to play a dogleg well because you need sound strategy and a clear plan of action.

Olympia Fields has three dogleg holes in a row—the second, third, and fourth—all curving to the right, and each with different problems to overcome. Number two measures 447 yards from the back tee, and the fairway runs roughly north and a bit east.

As we walk to the tee this autumn day, we'll notice that the wind is at our back at about fifteen miles an hour. That will cut my travel time from tee to green by adding another twenty to twenty-five yards to my drive.

Once we've recognized the wind factor, the next step is to size up the hole. I try not to dwell too much on what happens to bad shots; I devote my energy to planning good ones and trying to make them happen. Nevertheless, you can't totally ignore trouble.

This is a good place to put into practice some of the Packards' observations. As I look down the fairway, I first try to

spot the places that could present problems. This puts me in a position to judge the severity of penalty if I make an error. I absorb this information as part of my decision-making process.

On some doglegs, a player can go all out and attempt to shoot directly from tee to green. But that is rarely a good tactic, and if you are tempted to try it, recognize that it is usually a desperation gamble, and most of the time a foolhardy one.

Some conditions completely rule out such an attempt. If there are trees between you and your target and you can't shoot over them, there's no sense even trying.

But even assuming you hit a good shot that will give you a chance to clear those trees, you're still bucking tough odds: You are shooting blindly. You can't see the green, and failure almost certainly means a lost ball, or worse, a ball deep in the woods where even one shot won't get you out.

Take my word for it: There are times and places to take a gamble in golf, and cutting across a dogleg usually isn't one.

The advice the Packards gave us on how to play doglegs is sound. Your best strategy is to cut off as much of the "corner" as possible. That minimizes the actual distance from the tee to the green.

In most cases, the golf architect feels compelled to make you work for that shortcut. He designs trouble spots to penalize the poor shot.

As we've seen, trouble on a golf course comes in many forms, but the common location for hazards on a dogleg hole is at the bend where the fairway changes direction.

Trees are among the most troublesome of such hazards.

First, they effectively block off the side of the fairway on which they're located. If you fail to reach the turn, the trees will probably force you to make a second shot to open up the green. If you drive far enough, but off line, you may wind up in the woods and lose a stroke just getting back out onto the fairway.

Finally, if you try too hard to play safe by driving farther away from a cluster of trees than necessary, you'll have a more

difficult second shot and may need an extra stroke to reach the green.

There are also other dogleg hazards than trees; water hazards, fairway bunkers, rough, natural ravines, gullies, and similar features can all create penalties for the golfer who is careless or inaccurate on a dogleg hole.

As you plan your drive on a dogleg, then, you have to make a judgment. Can you or can't you drive through the elbow? Sometimes the answer is no.

If, for example, there is a fairway trap and your maximum shot won't carry it, you should examine the alternatives. And if there is water and the odds are against carrying it, you should certainly investigate some other pathway.

As the Packards point out, nearly every golf hole has more than one way to the cup.

As is so often the case, the choice of which way to take is a matter of individual decision. Since each player has his own skills and limitations, the important thing is to evaluate what you can do.

If you hit the ball 220 yards and there's a trap between 200 and 230 yards, you know you're not likely to hit the ball over it. As a matter of fact, a well-hit drive might land you in the sandpile, where you don't want to be.

By contrast, if you drive less than 200 yards consistently, that same trap could be a good target for you. You're not likely to reach it and it gives you something to aim for. In short, it is all up to you and your ability.

I want to stress, however, that you have to keep an open mind: to be able to adjust your game on the basis of how you're playing right now. You shouldn't lock youself into the notion that you're always going to hit a given club a set distance, because you aren't going to.

Don't become a prisoner of the tape measure and assume that you'll hit the same 200-yard shot today as you did the last time you played that same spot. There are just too many variables in golf to be able to know this.

To use but one illustration, a tail wind adds distance to your

shots. On a given day, a tailwind could change your game enough to make a favorable possibility of a shot that in headwind might force you to play safe.

Playing where the air is lighter, such as in Mexico or in the mountains, also adds distance to your drives; heavy wet air seems to take it away. Calculate those factors into your decision.

In the case of the second hole at Olympia Fields, the left hand side of the fairway is pretty wide open. The trouble occurs on the right, in the form of two traps about thirty yards apart. Between the two traps is rough.

In theory, the shortest distance to the green would require hitting a shot between those two traps. But that wouldn't really be a good gamble; it involves too much distance and too tight a fit. And even if you were successful, you'd wind up in the rough.

Another tactic for tackling this hole would be to use the first trap as a target and hook the ball back away from the bunker and into the fairway. That isn't a bad shot if you have pretty good control of your drive.

However, you will find there is an even better percentage shot.

Picture in your mind a golf hole that is a dogleg right. You'll see that a ball that hooks into the fairway has to come in at an angle, costing you about half the fairway as a target.

Worse, if you happen to hook a lot more than you intended, the ball can keep right on going through the fairway and into the rough on the opposite side.

Suppose, on the other hand, that the ball follows the fairway. As the fairway curves right, so does the ball. This situation gives you the most space on either side if your shot is somewhat off line. It also involves the shortest fairway distance between the tee and green, and while there is no sure way to guarantee a good drive, the ball that follows the fairway has the best chance of success and the maximum latitude for error.

The golfing term for that slight left-to-right movement of the ball is a "fade." In this case, a ball hit with a fade would fol-

But from a position standpoint, my shot wasn't all bad. In the left rough, I'm better off than I would have been trying to hit out of a trap.

I call this kind of shot a "bad" good shot—good in that it was planned correctly and for the proper part of the fairway, but bad because it landed in the rough rather than the fairway.

My problem now is basically the same one I faced on the first hole—a shot from the rough where it was impossible to control the spin on the ball. I'm confident the ball will go reasonably straight out of the thick grass, probably to a target area no bigger than thirty yards wide. My main concern is distance.

We've already established the general rule of not going over the green. And this holds especially true on the second at Olympia Fields because the green is pitched about 10 degrees from back to front.

As if that weren't enough, the cup today is in the rear; a shot over the green will compound my problems, forcing me to hit out of the rough behind the green onto a green slanted rear to front and with no place to putt the ball from which it won't roll too far.

In order to keep the ball from going over the green, I want to make sure I don't get it up into the air in the normal trajectory. If that happens, the wind, which is coming from behind me, may carry it too far.

All things considered, the correct shot is a three-quarter shot with a 6-iron that lands short of the green. This will slow the ball down enough to keep it from rolling over the green.

Had I been shooting from the fairway, I could have played aggressive golf. I would have gone on the offensive in my quest for a birdie by choosing my 5-iron for the remaining distance to the green. That club would have let me aim for the center of the green, confident that the backspin on the ball would stop it probably within three yards of where it hit.

From the rough, however, the ball can keep right on rolling because it has no backspin to stop it. I can't play aggressively; I've got to get the ball back into play. Under these circum-

stances, good strategy is to get the ball on the green in an area where you're not likely to three-putt.

That tactic—a drive, an approach, and two putts—gives you a par with an outside chance that you might can a long putt for a birdie.

On some later hole I may have a chance to pick the spot on the green where I'll have a comfortable level or uphill lie. Right now, I've got a much more fundamental objective: Simply to get the ball anywhere on the green, but no more than twenty-five feet away from the pin.

I accomplish this. The ball lands on the front of the green and rolls to the center. From there I lag a putt to within two feet of the pin and sink the follow-up for a par.

Another member of our foursome made the strategy error I mentioned earlier. He hit the ball down the right of the fairway and wound up in the rough to the right of the two bunkers. He hit a good shot, but because it was out of the rough, he couldn't control it. He went over the green, had an impossible chip shot coming back, and wound up with a bogey.

The third member of our group had the best drive. It was about the same distance off the tee as mine, but his ball was in the fairway. Then, however, he made a strategic error. He picked the wrong club and although his execution was good, he wound up at least thirty-five feet short of the pin and lost his chance at a birdie. That was lucky for us, since my partner didn't play the hole well at all.

Probably the toughest hole at Olympia Fields is the third, primarily because you are shooting for an elevated green. The hole is laid out with a high tee from which you shoot into a low fairway and then back up to a high green.

For a lot of reasons this is a difficult combination on any course.

If you're not careful you can be deceived by the distance to the green. If you shoot short, you have a difficult lie; you're on an upslope and the grass in front of the green usually grows to a height of three to five inches.

If you shoot long, on the other hand, you have the usual headache of overcoming the rough beyond the green and a renewed danger of overshooting coming back.

Just to add another problem, the third at Olympia Fields has two bunkers guarding the green.

The primary difficulty with an elevated green, however, is that you have to be more accurate in your approach shot. Unless you have great control, the height to the green takes away some of your option for a low shot. It is also more difficult for the ball to roll up onto the green; if you hit too hard, the ball will go over the green.

Normally, therefore, you have to play a more lofted club and attempt to put your ball well onto the green.

Earlier I described the third hole at Olympia Fields as one of a series of dogleg holes on the course, and to some golfers it appears that way. Actually it is pretty much a straightaway, but the green is set on a diagonal to the right, giving it some characteristics of a dogleg.

The third hole at Olympia Fields creates an excellent example of playing position golf. The green is very narrow and on an angle, so that if you're on the left, you have the length of the green to shoot for.

On the other hand, if your shot is from the right, the target is the width of the green, which makes it much shallower and gives you a much smaller target for keeping the ball on the putting surface.

It becomes a matter of percentages. If you are shooting for the shallow part of the green, your club selection is critical. If you have the length of the green, you have a greater margin of error; you can make a slight mistake—even be off by one club—and still wind up with the ball on the putting surface.

Recapping our plan, the correct drive is one down the left center of the fairway, so that your approach shot is into the open end of the green.

I have the right idea but fall into a common error. I'm thinking so much about hitting the ball to the left that I aim it too far in that direction. Coupled with that mistake, I have a

poorly timed swing. The result is the worst tee shot I hit all day.

I pull the ball so far left that it appears to be out-of-bounds and I hit a provisional ball off the tee. By rights I should have paid plenty for driving my first shot so poorly, but I got a break. I find that my ball apparently hit a tree branch, because it has stayed in bounds.

The ball landed in the left rough, but fortunately I have a clean shot for my approach to the green.

This second shot is the most important of the hole, because it determines how well you will score. A good approach provides the opportunity for a one-putt green; a poor approach substantially reduces the chance of making par.

From where my ball landed, I have a 170-yard uphill shot. Had the ball been in the fairway, I would have had a 6-iron shot; from the rough, I use a 7-iron.

Let me explain my choice of club. There is normally a ten-yard difference between one club and the next. From the same spot on the fairway, for example, a 6-iron will send a ball ten yards farther than a 7-iron. That same ten-yard difference will also hold when a player is hitting out of the rough.

Offhand, then, picking the shorter-distance club seems an odd choice. Why will the shorter-distance 7-iron carry as well from the rough as a 6-iron will from the fairway?

The difference is the spin on the ball.

When you hit out of the rough, the ball almost always has overspin or no spin at all, and almost always goes farther than it would from a fairway lie. Off the fairway, the ball has backspin and doesn't travel as far.

Because I'm hitting from the rough, I'm not sure what will happen with my approach shot. However, I do know what will happen if I go over the green—I'll have a bogey-5 for sure. On the other hand, even if I make a mistake and wind up short of the green, I still have a chance for a par.

Shooting short, however, poses some problems too. There is water twenty yards short of the green, and I have to clear it;

then I have to handle another potential problem. There is rough up the slope between the water and the green.

I decide that I have a thirty-foot landing area. If I come down fifteen feet short of the green I'll be in the rough, but will still have a respectable chip shot of fifteen feet onto the green that will leave room for the ball to roll safely.

Too short and I'd go into the water. And if I went beyond fifteen feet onto the green, there would be the danger of the ball going too far for lack of backspin to hold the green.

I hit the ball, but can't be sure of where it will land until I see it losing its trajectory; now I know my distance was reasonably close to being correct. The ball lands on the green and the forward slope of the green slows it down.

Even so, for lack of backspin the ball still rolls a full fifteen feet before it comes to a stop.

The pin is located in the rear of the green and I have a twenty-foot uphill putt. If you are going to make a mistake with a putt on an uphill green, make it on the short side of the cup; then your second putt will still be uphill.

My partner was a little inside me. Because we're playing a best-ball match, I let him putt first to give me an idea of the speed of the green.

I thought I had read it correctly, but whether from overconfidence or just carelessness I putt too strongly and the ball goes four feet past the pin. This leaves me with a curving right-to-left putt coming back, but fortunately I play it right to get my par.

This is only the third hole of the round, but already a pattern is developing. I am making mistakes—a bad drive and an approach putt that is too strong—but I am keeping the ball in play, where I have a chance to recover.

By contrast, one of our opponents is consistently hitting the ball down the right hand side of the fairway. On this hole he was on the right again, and it was obvious he had almost no chance of hitting the green because he didn't have a decent angle.

Sure enough, he hit the ball through the green and left him-

self a very difficult chip shot coming back. This creates a situation you encounter very often in golf. Once you get behind, the percentages change. It's almost as though you were digging your own hole deeper.

Our opponent's shots weren't those of a poor golfer. As a matter of fact, he had qualified for the national amateur and had placed first in a state tournament. Today, however, he has been starting his drives out to the right.

These weren't strategy errors; he simply hasn't been staying with his drive, and the ball has consistently gone down the right edge of the fairway or into the right rough—the wrong place to be.

Chapter 7

Playing One Shot at a Time

Let's take a brief timeout to put a perspective on our lesson.

We have now played three holes at Olympia Fields. Although Larry and Roger Packard didn't design this course, the basic principles they espouse are usable on any course, and we have been able to apply them in these opening holes.

For example, we've seen the importance of checking out the architecturally designed alternative routes to the green and have evaluated the path best suited to your game. We have also noted the special problems in and around the green created by the architect's design. These are the factors that require us to assess the risk-reward probabilities as we face each new hole.

I hope, too, that you are starting to look at each hole on your golf course through the eyes of its architect. If you can visualize the reasons for his design, you have the blueprint for playing it successfully.

Now let's take a look at some other subtleties of the game.

We have talked about some of the factors that influence how your course plays on a given day—the weather, wind, ground conditions, and time of day. We have also seen how different golf courses will present varying challenges depending upon the viewpoint of the architect.

There is still another ingredient. One of the most influential factors in how a golf course plays on a day-to-day basis is the

greenskeeper, or as he is more formally known, the golf course superintendent. His decisions can change an architect's plan, slow or speed greens, make the rough into a jungle, toughen up bunkers, and a lot more. Each greenskeeper approaches his task differently, and I'm sure you will find it valuable to get to know the greenskeeper at your course.

To give you an idea of the kind of questions you should ask and some hints on how to utilize their information, I'd like to introduce you to two of the top greenskeepers in the Chicago area—Oscar Miles and Randy Wahler. Oscar is the head man at Butler National, the giant toughie just west of Chicago and the home of the Western Open and Inter-Collegiate championships. Randy is in charge of Knollwood, a fine old club located north of Chicago.

Most golfers aren't likely to play on a course as demanding as Butler National and Knollwood. In part it is a matter of economics. It is a costly business to maintain a golf course in championship condition. It also takes the touch of an expert.

Miles and Wahler have different approaches to their task, partly based on the individual characteristics of their courses. Butler National is a course that plays to professional standards year 'round; Knollwood is primarily a membership course with the capability of being converted to a championship layout for special events.

Butler National is one of the courses we talked about earlier. It is 6,421-yards long and has three sets of tees. The gold tees are the forward ones; the white tees for better-than-average players add another 430 yards to the course; the blue championship tees produce a monster 7,733-yard course.

To give you an idea of its length, Pebble Beach measures only 6,800 yards long and Oakmont just under 7,000. Even the Western Open doesn't use the full length of Butler, instead limiting the par-3s to a series of 160-, 170-, 180-, and 190-yard holes.

Many golfers rate Butler difficult because it is long. I don't think it is length that makes it tough; I think it is the accuracy the course demands. It is one of the new courses—just about

twelve years old—but it was drawn up according to the specifications of the great courses of the early 1900s.

In its earlier days Butler National was criticized. The old Merion blue grass lay flat, and regardless of how close they cut it, still retained water. When you hit down into the grass you would get water on the clubface, and that had a tendency to make the ball lose spin.

But the folks who run Butler National have constantly improved it. They have cleared out a lot of the forest and changed the grass on all of the fairways so that it stands straight up. Probably the best description of Butler National is that it is very demanding. It is one of the few courses with a lot of hazards in the driving area. The out-of-bounds areas require accuracy off the tee, and if you hit an errant drive, you are likely to wind up with a double bogey and sometimes worse.

This is one reason why Andy Bean and Tom Weiskopf are just about the only long-ball hitters to win there. The accurate golfers—Tom Kite, Hale Erwin, and Bill Rogers—are the ones who play well at Butler. The same golfers who do well in the Open do well at Butler.

But distance is still important. The two major changes that convert an average golf course to a championship course are in the length of the holes and the height of the rough. For most tournaments the tees are set as far back as possible and the rough is allowed to grow.

Oscar Miles lets the Butler rough grow for the last three weeks before a tournament, and it is about four inches high when the shoot-for-money starts. That makes shooting from the rough like trying to hack your way through a jungle with a golf club.

Knollwood maintains its rough at about three-and-a-half inches high and raises it when the championship matches come to town. The taller rough and other changes probably add about three strokes to a good round at Knollwood.

I have mentioned the difficulties of the rough at Butler National, Knollwood, and other top golf clubs for a reason. You may never have the opportunity to play golf under tournament

conditions, but, wherever you play, it is essential that you understand the difference between the various kinds of rough you may encounter.

Many golfers, particularly those who play public courses, really have little experience with true rough. Public courses are designed for rapid play and the rough is likely to be simply poor quality grass or terrain that has been allowed to grow wild.

The rough you encounter in a tournament is designed to make you pay a penalty for missing the fairway. You obviously don't have as good a lie in the rough, so you can't control the ball as well. If you play on courses that have Bermuda grass, you may not be able to even see your ball. Bermuda grass tends to grow straight up and it can literally "hide" the ball.

But, whether it is Bermuda grass or creeping bent grass, the problem with shooting out of the rough is that the grass gets between your clubface and the ball and it has a tendency to make the ball "squirt" off the clubface without spin.

A second problem is that the thick rough may either cause the club to twist in your hands or it may give such resistance that it stops the clubhead. There was a famous TV closeup in the 1977 National Open at Pebble Beach in which Arnold Palmer was shown as he took a full swing out of the rough and the ball only traveled about eight feet. He probably had a bad lie to start with, but the rough was so difficult that even with his powerful hands and wrists, Palmer couldn't blast his way through the thick grass.

At Butler National, which maintains many of the Western Open standards throughout the year, the rough is the major concession to amateurs. For members, Miles keeps the rough cut at about two-and-a-half inches. That means that the golfer can at least find his ball most of the time, but it still makes getting out of the rough a tough golf shot for both pro and amateur.

If you are going to play golf for real, you should pay a penalty for getting into the rough, and Butler National gives the

golfer that challenge. He can play safe, pitch the ball out onto the fairway, and lose a stroke or take a gamble that he can control the shot out of the rough.

In dealing with hazards—and rough in particular—Oscar Miles has an interesting observation that I think applies to all golf courses. "As long as the good player doesn't make two bad shots in a row," says Miles, "he won't get above a bogey."

Under what circumstances are you likely to hit two bad shots in a row?

- By hitting your ball from the rough and flubbing the shot.
- By hitting your ball from the rough and squirting it across the fairway into the opposite rough.
- By hitting your ball from the rough to another position, still in the rough.

In general, any shot from the rough that doesn't get you back on the fairway is a second bad shot. If it seems likely that you're inviting a second bad shot in a row, don't take a chance; pitch the ball onto the fairway. That's good advice at Butler, and it's good advice on your course.

There are many arguments among golfers about whether Butler is too tough, particularly for the average golfer. I don't think so. In my opinion it is actually a very fair course *if*—and it's a big if—the golfer can stay in the fairway. The reason I think Butler is fair is that the fairways are as carefully manicured as the greens. The grass grows upright so that a ball, properly struck, gets good backspin and can hold the greens.

There is also a strip about twelve feet wide between the fairway and rough that is maintained at a height of one inch. It is not as difficult as the rough but not as easy as the fairway. If a golfer follows the rule of not making two bad shots in a row, he can still salvage a par from that semi-rough location.

One function of that intermediate rough is to help "define" the fairway. You may recall that Larry and Roger Packard believe in keeping their courses "fair." Greenskeepers have the

same thought. A golfer is entitled to fair notice of where trouble lies.

One way in which Miles gives such notice is with his lawnmowers. The fairways are mowed so that, even at a distance, it is obvious to the player where the fairway ends and the rough begins.

The resulting special areas are what architects and greenskeepers call "landing zones." They are the same areas in which golfers are expected to "land" their drives and, on longer holes, where their second shots are likely to end up.

When the pros are at Butler National, the landing zones are 250 to 280 yards from the tee. That's a good twenty or thirty yards farther away than the golf architects figure for even low handicap amateurs. The landing zones also toughen up the need for accuracy by providing a lot less real estate on either side of the fairway. At the landing zones the fairways are only about twenty-eight yards wide, and past that point are even narrower.

Under such conditions it obviously isn't all that easy to keep your shots in the fairway. To add to the difficulty, bunkers are located on the edge of the landing zone on the fourth, tenth, twelfth, fourteenth, and seventeenth holes. Combined with the narrower fairways, this provides a stiff test for the long-ball hitter. Unless he can keep his drive and fairway shots accurate, the extra length can become a liability.

Butler National also exacts a penalty for the careless player whose drive falls short of the landing area. His second shot can then enter the area of double-trouble—narrow fairways and bunkers.

Contour mowing is also a favorite tactic of Randy Wahler, the greenskeeper at Knollwood, another fine Chicago-area club. It can create the equivalent of doglegs in the fairway, and can also "toughen up" any hole by reducing the width of the fairway. The fairways at Knollwood average 100 feet, but with contour mowing can be flattened out for landing zones with narrowed stretches in between. Wahler has increased the chal-

lenge of one short par-4 hole by contouring the fairway down from 30 yards to 24 yards wide around the landing zone.

The challenge on any topflight golf course is the quality of the greens. Butler National has all the characteristics of a championship layout. In addition, its greens place a special demand on the golfer; they run diagonal to the direction of the fairways. As a result, their front-to-back width is narrow, forcing the player to be very precise with his approach shot.

Nevertheless, there are some concessions that offset these difficulties. Butler National is very well marked and there are fairway locations clearly identified with the yardage to the green. There is also an extra not found at many clubs. Players are furnished with a yardage book giving the layout of each green and telling them how far it is from the edge to the middle of the green.

What it doesn't tell them is that the greens are fast. You and I know whether a green is fast or slow by how far the ball rolls after we hit with our putter. But at tournament time, the "speed" of the green is determined with a machine that rolls a golf ball down an incline and measures the number of feet the ball rolls. During year-round play, Butler greens measure a 9 on the speed scale; at tournament time they measure 10 to 10½.

This means that a putt hit hard enough to roll nine feet during regular play will roll ten to ten-and-a-half feet in tournament play. Thus, while you have to draw an accurate line when putting at Butler, your putts will also keep on going if you don't have the right touch. Moreover, those slick greens challenge your chip and approach shots. You've got to get good backspin on your iron shots to keep the ball from running too far.

Randy Wahler is another believer in firm, fast greens. Before one national amateur tournament he put forty pounds of bricks in his mowers, rolled them every other day and double-cut the greens. It brought the green speed up to an 11.

Greens get a lot of wear because the traffic on them is concentrated in the relatively small area around the pins. For this reason, the placement of the pins is changed daily so that each area gets a "rest." Miles divides his greens into six segments,

going clockwise: two front, two middle, and two back. And when the flags are moved, so are the tees, so that each hole plays the same distance every day.

Wahler also divides his greens into six sections, using a different one each day. He also keeps his rotation sequence secret from the players, so they can't anticipate too well where the pin will be.

For all the attention given the fast greens and the difficult rough at Butler, it is the wind that seems to affect scores the most. Butler does not have the tree-lined fairways of some of the old, classic courses. As a result, it is a panoramic golf course but is open to a wind that can come from almost any direction.

The course record, a 64, was set when the course was in excellent condition and the golfer had an outstanding day. But the biggest contributor was probably the fact that on that particular day there was little wind.

Regardless of circumstances, however, sub-par rounds at Butler come hard. In theory, the player with the natural fade has an advantage because of the layout of the dogleg holes. But in the opinion of Oscar Miles it is accuracy, rather than a natural fade or the ability to hit the long ball that wins championships at Butler.

The rough and the fast greens will catch up to the scrambler. For example, a golfer may be under par after playing the first six holes but then come the seventh, eighth, and ninth. A few mistakes, a slight loss of concentration, and a bit of overconfidence and the golfer is no longer under par; he's winding up the front nine with a 40.

Even the long-ball hitters can't reach green on the par-5 seventh hole in two. And even though it draws the most strokes, it isn't the toughest hole on the front nine; that honor goes to the ninth hole, which has an out-of-bounds area, measures 431 yards, and requires a very precise shot off the tee.

It is on the tee shot that Miles believes most professional golfers are likely to err in playing Butler National. In his opinion, the smart player keeps his driver in the bag and instead

chooses a No. 1 iron on at least four holes—ninth, fifteenth, sixteenth, and eighteenth. On all four, Miles feels this club provides sufficient distance to put the ball in the best position to reach the green.

On most golf courses the finishing holes are the most challenging. That's true at Butler where the seventeenth encourages a golfer to try for maximum distance. If he's a non-hooker and comes down on the right, he can usually reach the green.

In 1974 Tom Weiskopf lost the Western Open at Butler on the seventeenth and eighteenth holes. He drove too far on seventeen and wound up with a shot blocked by the pumphouse that forced him to chip out. He bogeyed the hole. Then on eighteen, he hit too far to the right and landed by a creek. At that point he had lost a tournament that just about everybody had conceded to him—an illustration of the treachery of final holes.

The closing hole at Butler also underscores Oscar Miles' comment that, long as his course is, it sometimes penalizes the long-ball hitter. A ball hit too far on the eighteenth at Butler is likely to land in a place where the trees interfere with the shot to the green.

This last hole at Butler is particularly demanding because it is contradictory. The fairway position requires a fade, but the green—which is on a diagonal—calls for a slight draw. The ball must go left of center and not be too long for the player to get in good pin position. It is small wonder that this hole has played a key role in the outcome of so many tournaments.

Just as the closing holes cost Weiskopf the Western Open in 1974, eight years later they won it for him. He was down one stroke to Larry Nelson, who had led all the way. Nelson hit his tee shot into the intermediate rough on the right side of eighteen. Just as Nelson was preparing to shoot, the fans got noisy and he had to step away from the ball. This probably cost him his concentration, at least momentarily. When he finally was able to hit his second shot, it didn't carry, landing on the apron of the green.

Weiskopf's drive was in the middle of the fairway. In order

to have a chance to catch Nelson, he had to put his approach shot inside that of his opponent. Tom was good for the challenge. He hit a fabulous approach shot. Miles calls it "the greatest shot I ever saw at Butler." It hit right at the pin and then rolled back about six feet from backspin.

That shot turned the game around. Now the pressure was on Nelson. He chipped short and then missed his putt; Weiskopf didn't, and wound up the Western Open champion.

Many of today's golf-playing greenskeepers, like Randy Wahler, carry a low handicap, in part because they have an edge. As Wahler says about Knollwood, "I know the contours better than most golfers because I know the drainage. I know how the water flows on the course, I know the wet spots, the dry spots. I know particular locations where the ball isn't going to roll at all because there's a very soft spot there."

And he adds, "I can anticipate variances in the speed of the greens because I know the amount of clippings we're getting. I know when greens are fast because we have just top dressed and verticut them." That's not boasting, it's his job. But it also happens to pay off when he gets a chance to play a round. And while you probably won't have access to all that inside information when you play, you can note from Randy Wahler some of the places to watch.

Randy also has some playing advice worth heeding:

"The tough shot in golf is the chip around the green. On fast greens chip shots are very demanding and that's where your average player has a lot of difficulty. By contrast, a good player knows how to chip not only with the pitching wedge but also by using a sand wedge. He knows how to use it to pitch the ball even out of little longer grass."

Store away Randy Wahler's advice for later use. Now, what about Oscar Miles. How can you apply his views to your game?

- First, be alert to the condition of the golf course, particularly the greens.

127

- Two, avoid making two bad shots in a row. That's where the score starts to mount.
- Three, even though length plays a big role in your score, the person who places his shots best will usually outdo the long hitter.
- Fourth, important as the course conditions are, none rank with the need to avoid errors.

I asked Oscar Miles what he thought was the greatest single mistake players make on a golf course.

His reply: "Their biggest mistake is remembering the previous shot. If they three-putt a green they're worried about the next green. You've got to forget that and wait to the practice green after the round. There's only one way to play good golf. One shot at a time."

Chapter 8

Mastering the Uphill Lie

Now on to Hole No. 4.

Our first hole at Olympia Fields presented the problem of an out-of-bounds area on the left, the second was a dogleg, and the third was a challenging elevated green. Now we face the toughest tee shot on the course—one that doesn't give you much tolerance on either side.

The fourth hole at Olympia Fields is about 390 yards long and, like the first, has an out-of-bounds on the left. But unlike the first hole, which was comparatively open, the fourth has a lot of trees on the right. As a result, the fairway is a tight one that demands accuracy in order to stay out of trouble.

You can't favor the left side of the fairway because it isn't open; and you can't favor the right side because it isn't open either. There is only one way to play this hole well. You must hit a good tee shot, and that means hitting it down the middle of the fairway.

Your position when you address the ball is called your "setup." Setup is simply a term meaning how you position yourself when you address the ball. It is how you stand to the ball, how you position your feet and body to aim the ball, etc. Every golfer has his own individualized setup. Lee Trevino, for example, when he sets up looks like he is going to hit the

ball 50 yards to the left of the target. However, when he starts his backswing, you can see his shoulders move to the right which brings his swing into the proper arc. Each golfer has his own mannerisms which help him feel comfortable. My setup differs from that of most golfers. Except when I want to hit a fade, I usually tee up the ball on the left side of the driving area.

I am not suggesting that you follow my example. There isn't any reason for you to follow it; it simply helps me set up the hole better in my mind.

If my swing is in the groove, that left-side setup works for me; the ball heads away from the target and then draws back into the zone where I want it to land.

As you'll recall, that has been my tactic on every hole except the second. On that hole, instead of setting up left, I teed up in the center of the driving area because the hole was a dogleg to the right.

My tee shot on the fourth hole is just what I wanted it to be—low, hard, and with a slight draw on the ball. The ball ends up right where it belongs—on the left side of the fairway.

There is only one hitch.

I've mentioned before that you are almost always better off in the fairway than in the rough or a hazard. But as I've also said, landing in the fairway doesn't always guarantee a good lie.

In this case the ball ends up on an uphill lie. This is always a troublesome shot because it is hard to gauge the distance your ball will travel on the next shot. The arc of your swing is different than it would be on a level fairway, and when you hit the ball it shoots into the air with a higher trajectory than usual.

Suffice it to say that there are many ways you can go wrong when you have an uphill lie. One common mistake is swinging too hard. Because it is harder to keep your balance when the ground is uneven, an uphill lie is one place where you should deliberately slow down your swing.

Another way to go wrong is to fail to shift your weight.

On any good shot, you wind up with your weight on your

left side. But when you're shooting from an uphill lie, that becomes very difficult to do, and if you aren't careful, your weight stays on your right and you pull the ball.

In addition to swinging too hard or failing to shift your weight, there are other common mistakes made on an uphill lie. When you don't have a level lie, you aren't in control of the shot; you have a tendency to "scoop" the ball.

This problem occurs most frequently with wedge shots, particularly in the hands of a golfer inexperienced with this club. The reason? He doesn't trust the loft of the club and tries to "help" the ball into the air.

When a golfer doesn't allow the loft of the club to do the work on an uphill lie, the usual result is a real "fat" hit—one that comes down behind the ball—and a shot that falls far short of where it was intended to.

Club selection is another factor. Usually when I have an uphill lie, or a sidehill lie where the ball is higher or lower than my feet, I take a longer club than usual. By longer club, we mean a club which would carry the ball farther; e.g., using a 5-iron instead of a 6. The reason: the uphill lie means the ball goes higher in the air as compared to a shot off level ground and consequently doesn't travel as far.

Because of the tendency to "scoop," you are likely to lose distance from an uphill lie. For example, you may hit an 8-iron shot only the distance you would normally hit a 9-iron.

Had I had a level lie on the fairway, I would have used a 9-iron. With my uphill lie, however, a 9-iron will leave me short. I choose an 8-iron.

It was probably a good club selection, but I make a serious mental blunder. I do not approach the shot with confidence; I have some doubt about how to play the ball, and it shows in the result.

Instead of coming down on the front edge of the green, as I planned, the ball goes much farther than I wanted—about forty feet beyond the pin. It is, pure and simple, a bad golf shot.

The reason for it was bad golf technique.

I was afraid that the uphill lie would make me pull the ball,

and intended to hit it more softly in order to get the correct line to the pin. Instead, I hit it too full and it overshot the mark.

Not only did I hit a poor shot, but with that shot I also reversed my percentages. It was almost as though I had hit a poor drive and then had to play my second shot out of the rough—it erased the effect of my good drive.

Had I hit a fairly decent second shot, I would now have a reasonable chance for a birdie putt. Instead, I had to cover a long, tough downslope, which means that I now have to make two good putts to get down in par.

Fortunately for my score, I make up for the poor approach shot by hitting an excellent putt from the back of the green to within two feet of the cup, and I wind up getting my par.

My partner had trouble all the way. He hit out of bounds off the tee, then hit the ball into a bunker, left it in the bunker on his next shot, and then pitched his fourth shot past the hole.

My chief opponent again hit to the right, this time into the trees, and put his second shot into a trap. He made a reasonably good escape, but two-putted. His partner also hit long to the green and was even farther from the cup than I was. He hit a fantastic putt, but lost his advantage by taking two more putts to can the ball.

Chapter 9
Estimating the Wind

The fifth hole at Olympia is a lesson in the importance of keeping the ball in play. It is a short hole, about 330 yards, but there are trees on both the right and left sides.

I'm not talking about trees so thick that you hit the ball and an Indian brings it back. Nor am I talking about terrain with just an occasional tree. I'm talking about a type of hole you too are likely to encounter, with a lot of good-sized trees and the problems they provide for the golfer.

The trees on the right are the same ones that line the rough on the fourth hole. The trees on the left aren't quite as thick, but there's a trap to add to the potential problems on that side.

In fact, the fifth hole at Olympia Fields is such a challenge that during the Western Open, a lot of players hit an iron from the tee rather than take a chance on a drive that might go off line into the woods.

There can be another advantage in using an iron—for an unusual reason. It can make the second shot easier. The pro with a long tee shot will probably be faced with a three-quarter approach to the green; the one who hits shorter off the tee will have a full wedge shot, which is usually easier to spin and stop than the three-quarter shot.

No matter how you play this or any other hole, trees can be a real concern to your game. A tree can give you two distinct and different problems. If your ball lands up against a tree or where there are low overhanging branches, there may not be room to

swing your club, e.g., every once in a while you see a golfer who has to turn his club upside down and swing left handed because there is no other way to reach his ball. That's one kind of problem. A second is where there is a tall tree and there isn't room to either clear it overhead or a suitable shot under or through the tree.

Of course it is also possible to land in the woods and have a free swing and enough room to maneuver the ball around the trees and on the way toward the hole. But it just doesn't seem to happen that way very often.

Most often when you get into a tight lie with a tree, your swing is locked up, and you have to improvise some way to strike the ball, even hitting it backhand on occasion.

If you play fairly regularly, that problem can occur often enough to make practicing such a shot worthwhile. There is no magical way to do it; just take one of your straighter irons, turn it around, and swing it from the other side.

There are also some commonsense things you can do. Take your time. Get a good balance. Finally, don't try to be a hero; just get the ball out of trouble and into a place where you can get a decent shot.

The same advice applies when you have the super-problem of both a stymied swing and blocked shot. You can't swing naturally and there is really no good path for the ball to follow.

This is one of the most difficult shots for any golfer, not because it requires skill (there often isn't much you can do), but because it requires the player to go against his competitive instincts.

The golfer thinks—incorrectly—that he is conceding defeat; that he is "losing ground" because he isn't heading directly for the green. That's a mistake you shouldn't make if you have developed good thinking habits.

Remember Oscar Miles' theory, and don't let one bad shot cost you two. Remember also that you'll be bucking tremendous odds if you blindly push ahead on every shot. Not only will you lessen your chances for a par, but you'll probably be inviting a bogey or double bogey.

If, on the other hand, you can pitch the ball out onto the fairway, you still have a chance for a good third shot and a par.

Fortunately, I don't run into any such problems.

I play the fifth hole right out of the book. I have complete control on my tee shot and hit it straight down the middle of the fairway. When you hit them that way, trees are just a pleasant part of the scenery.

My drive not only goes down the middle of the fairway, but leaves me only about ninety yards from the green. My wedge shot lands just three feet from the pin and I make my putt.

Three good shots in a row! I'm on top of the world.

A major change in our game is going to occur as we tee off on the 6th tee. Up until now the wind has not had a major effect on our game. Now, for the first time, it will play a key role in club selection and the accuracy with which we shoot for the green. So let's take time out to study wind and its influences on our play.

Just about every sports fan is aware of the importance of the wind. It is tougher to hit home runs against the wind, harder for the quarterback to control his passes. Even though a golf ball is much smaller than a baseball or football, it is still subject to all the laws of aerodynamics. As every golfer knows, a golf ball isn't going to travel quite the same way on a windy day as when there is no wind.

Let's start out with some elementary facts about playing under wind conditions. Before you can determine the effect of wind on your shots, you must first decide just how hard the wind is blowing.

Fortunately for all golfers, a seagoing man had the same concern. Back in 1805, Sir Francis Beaufort, a British Rear Admiral, needed to know the effect of wind on his country's sailing ships, and devised the scale that bears his name.

Here for the benefit of golfers is an updated version of the Beaufort scale.

- If you can see smoke in your vicinity and it is rising straight up, there is virtually no wind.

- When the smoke is drifting lazily with the air, the wind is probably only a one- or two-mile-per-hour wind.
- When you can feel the wind on your face, and the leaves are rustling, this is a light breeze of probably between four and seven miles an hour.
- If the wind is strong enough to move leaves and small twigs, it is labeled a "gentle breeze" and probably clocks in at eight to twelve miles an hour. When small tree branches sway and dust and loose paper blows around, the wind is considered a "moderate" breeze and registers somewhere between thirteen and eighteen miles an hour.
- A "fresh" breeze, which can sway small trees, travels at a speed of nineteen to twenty-four miles an hour.
- If the wind is powerful enough to sway large tree branches, it is considered a "strong" breeze. That's about twenty-five to thirty-one miles an hour.

Above that figure, the winds are strong enough to be considered a gale, and it is highly unlikely you will—or should—be on the golf course.

Now that we have a way to determine approximately how strong the wind is at any given time, let's find out how it affects the golf ball, and how much you must allow for windage when you are planning your shots.

I talked to Tom Hardman who heads an operation for the Wilson Sporting Goods Company in Palm Beach Gardens, Florida and knows as much about golf balls and wind conditions as any person I know.

Wilson has several facilities on the site, including a fifty foot wind tunnel. But the most interesting experiments take place inside a twenty-five foot square building equipped with a regulation tee and a machine named "Iron Byron," which is designed after the golf swing of Byron Nelson, one of the all time greats of the game.

Iron Byron simulates the human golfer but with a great deal more consistency. It hits golf balls through two large open doors onto a fairway, which is mowed and maintained to golf

club standards. The fairway is measured in a series of grids from 130 yards to 300 yards so every shot is charted for trajectory, velocity of the clubhead, roll, left and right movement, and a host of other tests involving golf ball behavior.

In addition to the golf machine, golfers are also brought in to use the facilities so their shots can be compared to those of Iron Byron. Wilson chose this site partly because there is no wind in the morning, which eliminates this variable. At the same location, however, there is wind in the afternoon, and it is used in testing just what happens to a golf ball under various wind conditions.

Wilson is not unique in studying the aerodynamics of golf balls. All major ball manufacturers are studying how changes in the "dimples" on a golf ball can make it fly truer to its target.

This is such a significant project that Wilson has even used General Dynamics Corporation's wind-tunnel facilities in California to help design the golf balls its advisory staff uses on the tour.

As Tom Hardman points out, not all golf balls act alike in the wind. The best way to find this out is to experiment with various golf balls yourself under similar wind conditions, and note the differences.

If you want to generalize, states Hardman, all golf balls, regardless of their maker, will behave in a similar manner when hit directly into the wind. It is when the wind is blowing across the fairway that the greatest differences in golf balls show up.

First let's consider a shot directly into the wind. According to Tom Hardman's research, even a gentle breeze can have a major influence on your shot. As a rule of thumb, you will lose a yard and a half of distance for every mile per hour the wind is blowing. This means that if you can reach the green of a par-3 with a 7-iron on a windless day, you will fall six to ten yards short of that when shooting into even a light breeze.

A gentle to moderate breeze could take as many as twenty yards off your distance. To make up those "lost" yards, you probably should discard the 7-iron in favor of a 6-iron.

If you are hitting with the wind, you reverse the process. Every mile per hour ADDS a yard-and-a-half to your shots. In a light breeze, you would get another ten yards and therefore in a gentle to moderate breeze you should probably go down one club to an 8-iron instead of a 7-iron.

Obviously, the yardage will to some extent depend on the golfer. According to Tom Hardman, the figures given above hold up pretty well regardless of which club is used or how far the golfer hits with it.

In practical terms, this means that you can add a yard-and-a-half to your distance with any club when the wind is behind you—ten yards in a light breeze; twenty when the wind is strong enough to sway small tree limbs.

What about crosswinds?

This is the critical test for a golf ball. If the ball holds its line well, winds that blow across the fairway will have less impact on its flight than either a head or tail wind. But remember, not all golf balls hold the line well.

The best balls will average about a yard of yaw per mile-an-hour of crosswind. This can vary considerably with the characteristics of the golf ball you use.

Remember, though, that you have only a limited left-to-right tolerance on most shots and that if you don't allow for wind, you can miss the green with a perfectly respectable tee shot on a par-3 hole, and a fairly strong breeze can take a shot aimed down the fairway and blow it into the rough.

I suggest you memorize Tom Hardman's rule: every mile-per-hour of headwind will take a yard-and-a-half off your distance, every mile per hour of tailwind will add a yard-and-a-half, and every mile per hour of crosswind will send your ball one yard to the side. Change those numbers, if you have to, to accommodate your brand of golf ball and your style of play.

And don't forget, winds shift and so does the direction of the holes on any golf course. That's what we're going to find as we go to the sixth hole at Olympia Fields.

* * *

The sixth hole at Olympia Fields is a special favorite of mine. I have made twelve hole-in-one shots in my life and one was on this hole. That was back in 1968, but you never forget the perfect shot.

This hole can provide you with a lot of valuable golf information. To play it correctly, you must be able to estimate distance, allow for the wind, and properly utilize the tee.

On the sixth hole you tee off from an elevated area and shoot down into the green. In front of the green and to the left is a small creek that meanders through the course.

First, let's talk about distance.

On this hole there is no problem. The permanent markers measure to the middle of the green. On this day the pin is about in the middle, so I can use the distance on the marker.

Otherwise you have to adjust, depending on the pin location. I don't have the yardage marked off, so I have to estimate.

Under such circumstances, I usually divide the green into quarters, and estimate in which quarter the pin is located. That gives me an approximation of the distance from the tee to the cup. It isn't exact, of course, but close enough.

The green is approximately seventeen yards wide and thirty yards deep. And the pin is just right of center, about 150 yards from the tee.

Today the sixth hole will play tough because we are heading into a south wind, which will also face us on the next four holes. The size of the green makes my drive a very demanding shot, and even if I place the ball well the pin is located in an area where there are a number of undulations.

Now for my choice of club.

Most often when I play this hole I use an 8-iron, but the wind is blowing at about twenty miles an hour and so I opt for a 6-iron. Actually I have two options: I can choose between a hard 7-iron and an easy 6-iron shot.

My choice is the 6-iron, and here's why.

I don't want to swing too hard when I'm shooting into the wind. The harder you swing, the higher the ball goes. You are

striking the ball with a more downward blow, and it shoots the ball into the air more quickly, giving it a higher trajectory.

There are two reasons why I don't want to get the ball up any higher than necessary.

First, I want to keep the ball low because I am shooting from an elevated tee down into the green. Second—and especially in a situation like this—a ball that is up in the air is at the mercy of the wind.

Therefore, when you're shooting into the wind, the normal rule is to use more three-quarter shots and hit the ball more softly.

It is also essential to tee up the ball. That sounds very elementary, but not all golfers follow that advice. Some think it is a good idea to play tee shots off the ground when they're using the lofted, short-distance clubs. Presumably, they feel this will give them a better "bite," and their shot will hold the green better.

But that's not the way to do it.

The remedy for a shot that doesn't have backspin isn't to give up the tee and shoot off the ground. That's a mistake. It isn't the lie that makes the difference. The average golfer fails to get backspin primarily because he forgets one thing: That he shouldn't swing differently just because the ball is on a tee.

As for whether to use a tee or not, if you stop and think about it, the very best lie you are going to get on a golf course is a ball on the tee. It doesn't make sense not to take advantage of that fact, does it?

I tee the ball up, and hit a fabulous iron shot. I must have followed my own advice: my shot had the right line of flight; I allowed for the wind; and I picked the right club for the distance. The ball lands just two feet from the cup and pulls back to about seven feet.

I almost pull off a second great shot. My putt heads straight for the cup but doesn't drop in, and I had to settle for a par.

The next hole—the seventh at Olympia Fields—is one that shows how the wind can change the character of a hole. It is a

par-4 dogleg left and about 410 yards long. If there is no wind or if the wind is behind you, this is considered an easy hole.

But when you play into the south wind on the seventh, it becomes a difficult hole, and that's the situation today. The wind is out of the south, and that makes the hole "play long."

As we always do, we'll first look at the trouble areas. On our left there are trees. On the right there are two traps. The entranceway to the green is on the right, so that is the general area in which we would like the ball to wind up.

The ideal drive will start out toward those traps on the right, but then draw back into the fairway. That is my intention, and my drive does start out to the right, but instead of drawing back into the fairway, it comes down in the right rough.

This was another error, but fortunately not a strategic one. The ball is in the part of the golf course from which I still have my best percentage shot to the green.

And I take advantage of it. I'm able to hit the ball out of the rough and still control the distance enough that my shot lands on the green. But you almost always pay a penalty for wandering off the fairway, and that's what happened to me.

Even though the ball landed on the green, it had that familiar shortcoming of shots out of the rough—little or no backspin.

I had the right line and the right distance. Had my drive stayed in the fairway, I might have been able to put my approach shot close enough to the pin for a birdie putt. Instead, I overshot the cup and it takes me two putts to finish out the hole.

I suppose you shouldn't complain when you have to "settle" for a par. After all, that's the standard on which golf is based. But making and not making birdies is what distinguishes good golfers from champions.

If you're going to attempt to play topflight golf, the stroke you don't pick up can count almost as much as one you lose through an error. And even if your scores aren't yet challenging par, I want you to get into the habit of thinking like a pro.

The eighth hole at Olympia Fields is an excellent example of a "fair" hole. It is a par-3 hole, 230 yards to the green. That's

a pretty challenging tee shot, complicated by a large trap in front of the green.

However, the architect has made the eighth a fair hole by creating a green large enough to be a good target. A short while ago we played the sixth hole, where the green was about thirty yards by seventeen yards deep; the eighth green is probably thirty yards wide by forty yards deep.

The sixth hole was shorter, and it was reasonable to expect a golfer to reach the green—which is also a fair one—with his tee shot. The eighth green is more demanding, but the architect has "evened up" the difference in distance between the two holes by increasing the target area.

The larger green means the golfer can "go for it" off the tee with some degree of confidence that the ball will land on the green and not roll off. The more cautious golfer can shoot short and have an invitingly large target for his approach.

On this day, the eighth hole has changed character because of the wind. On most days I will hit a 3-wood shot about 250 yards, which would normally be too much for this 230-yard hole.

But today I am hitting into the wind, and the 3-wood is the right club. My tee shot lands on the green, leaving me about a twenty-five-foot putt. Those are the kind of putts that nobody makes consistently; however, they are the putts that a golfer with a "hot hand" can sink.

I do half the job well; I have the right distance for the putt. However, I stroke it poorly. I pull it and the ball goes about a foot-and-a-half to the left of the cup.

Once more I am playing good golf but not great golf. My approach putt met a basic criterion: I got the ball within a three-foot circle of the cup and so was able to sink the second putt for another par.

But had I been just a little bit more accurate on my stroke, I would have had a bonus—a birdie putt.

I have a similar opportunity on the ninth green, but make another putting error—this time slightly overestimating the distance to the cup.

The ninth hole at Olympia Fields is a long and difficult one. It measures a good 430 yards, and the green is well trapped on both sides. As you know, tournaments save the toughest holes for last if they can.

When the PGA tournament was held here in 1961, the ninth hole was redesignated as the final, eighteenth hole. Older golfers will remember that tournament because it was on this green that Jerry Barber sank a fantastic putt to defeat Don January.

Today I am playing this hole in near-championship form myself. I hit an excellent drive and a good iron shot to take me within twenty feet of the cup. I stroke my putt right on line and it hits the middle of the cup, but doesn't go in, instead hitting the back of the cup and bouncing out. The reason? I had just a little too much speed on the putt. For the third hole in a row, I had a chance for a birdie but didn't make it.

Chapter 10

Conquering the
Water Hazards

We are now halfway through our round of golf, and I'm playing a pretty consistent game.

Mid-round can be a letdown time if you aren't careful. Frequently a foursome takes a break after the ninth green for a drink and a snack. It is also a time when the scorekeeper tabulates the strokes for each golfer.

Whether you have a friendly wager going or are competing for your own satisfaction, you face the same kind of problem you faced on your opening tee shot.

If you are down a few strokes to your opponents, there is a tendency to press, not only in the wagering but in your game. You are behind and you want to catch up.

On the other hand, if you are up on your rivals, it is easy to start looking ahead to the eighteenth hole and forget that you still have plenty of golf to play before you get to the clubhouse.

I don't have to mention the problems of too much food or liquid in your system after the mid-round break, but it is worth commenting on "cooling off." If your stopover between the ninth green and tenth tee is only a matter of a few minutes, your muscles don't have much chance to tighten up.

But it is another matter if you take a full-fledged stop for lunch or if the course jams up so that you're delayed getting back into play on the tenth tee. Under these conditions it is a

good idea to take a few extra swings with an iron or a wood to limber up once again and remind your body of the task ahead.

It will also help you get back your golf concentration. You'll need it for the nine holes still left to play.

Except for out-of-bounds areas, probably no hazard on the golf course strikes more terror into the amateur than water. Some golfers seem to find even small rain puddles on the fairway.

For this reason there are people who make a living, and a pretty good one at that, operating concessions to salvage golf balls from water hazards. Yet the fact is that most water holes are more a mental hazard than a physical one.

The tenth hole at Olympia Fields illustrates this point. There is a small pond on the right, which any halfway decent shot should avoid. It still snares a lot of golf balls, however, for one simple reason: golfers turn it into a major mental hazard.

How do you avoid this problem?

Your first task is to evaluate all possible sources of trouble on the hole, including water. If there is a river, a creek, a pond, a lake, or any other water hazard, landing in it can cost you a penalty stroke.

The trick is to separate the real danger of the hazard from the imagined danger.

A hazard that lies in your target area and may snare a shot that falls short, strays too far left or right, or doesn't go quite where you want it to for some other reason is a legitimate reason for caution.

There are many golf holes with hazards of this kind. Pebble Beach is an example of a course where an error can put your ball in the ocean or down in a deep ravine where it is essentially lost.

You have to play these genuinely troublesome water holes according to your talents. You gamble where you have to and play safe where you have to, just as you would with a tough trap or a thickly wooded hazard.

There are many water hazards, however, that don't deserve that much attention, and which most good golfers can ignore.

Yet both important and incidental water hazards can play havoc with the uncertain golfer, and this is particularly true of beginners who find water just ahead of them when they get to the tee.

Even a water hazard that is only a few yards across can constitute a major block in the golfer's thinking process. He becomes so concerned about shooting over it that he loses concentration and rhythm in his swing.

The result is often a topped shot or a flubbed shot that does go in the water.

When that happens a few times, the golfer is likely to develop a habit of reaching into his bag for a cut up or battered ball—virtually conceding that he is going to mess up the shot.

That's a bad habit, and if you've fallen into it, you should learn to conquer that fear now. Here's how I think you can do it.

- First, learn to ignore any water hazard that is not a legitimate threat. If it can't bother you, don't you bother with it.
- Second, pick out a target area where you'd like your ball to go.
- Third, select the club that will let you reach your target without undue pressure.
- Fourth, concentrate on your target area and attempt to block everything else out of your mind. Get your stance set, your goal in mind, and your attention focussed on your objective.
- Fifth, shift your full attention to the ball.
- Sixth, begin your "takeaway" smoothly, and swing the club as you would for a comparable shot anywhere else on the fairway.

By devoting your full attention to a target area and then shifting your concentration to the golf ball, you are effectively

"ignoring" the water hazard and swinging naturally as though it weren't there.

In golf, as in business, nothing succeeds like success. I believe that any golfer who follows this formula can develop confidence in his ability to hit the ball under pressure. It is the best antidote I know for water-jitters.

Once you see the tenth hole at Olympia Fields in perspective, you see that the water hazard isn't really the challenge—that it is instead the dogleg left. The tenth hole is about 420 yards long; but today we have made the turn and the wind is at our back, and so the hole plays shorter.

I follow my customary routine. I tee up on the left, aim right, and plan to hit a drive that will draw back into the fairway. I hit a good shot, but this is an instance where inches count. My ball ends up just about a foot into the right rough.

I am now about 150 yards out, which would be a 7-iron shot for me on a windless day. However, because the wind is behind me I take off two clubs and hit a 9-iron on my second shot.

Even with this my shot is too strong. The ball goes past the cup by twenty-five feet. But I am lucky. On most greens that would leave a tough downhill putt coming back. However, the tenth green is an exception; there is a slope in the front, but beyond it the green is as flat as a tabletop.

I am "thinking" downhill, however, because I "baby" my lag putt. As a result it is weak and I leave myself a four-foot second putt. Straining my odds, I make the putt and can mark another par on my scorecard.

Every once in a while, somebody will ask if I ever deliberately aim to put my ball in a bunker. The answer is "yes," but only rarely. I remember playing Pebble Beach in the 1972 Open when the greens were so slick that it took an almost perfect shot to hold them.

In that case it was a better percentage shot to land in the bunker ahead of the green than to take a chance of overshooting.

That, however, was a very unusual situation. Even the most

confident wedge player would prefer not to be in sand if he can avoid it. Yet you sometimes wind up in a bunker accidentally and it turns out to be preferable to other nearby lies.

Today, on the eleventh hole at Olympia Fields, I don't land in a trap, but would have been better off if I had.

The eleventh is another hole that sets up to the right and then doglegs left. I hit a bad tee shot—a low pull—and my ball lands in the rough just about midway between two traps.

Had I landed in either trap I would have had a more manageable second shot; as it is, having landed in the rough I have the usual problem of having to control my distance.

But it works out all right.

Somehow I get spin into the ball and, instead of running some twenty-five feet after it lands, its stops after about eight feet, and I'm able to avoid any additional problems on the green.

The next hole, the twelfth, has a little bit of everything—a tight fairway, trees on both sides, a water hazard, and a fairway bunker.

Let's take the problems in reverse order. The bunker is about 260 yards out, and that comes within my driving range, making it possible that my ball will wind up there. You don't hit bunker shots too often, but it is a good idea to know how to play them if you do.

As usual, you must first consider safety. If you encounter a fairway bunker with a high lip, it may be too big a gamble to try a wood or a long iron. You then have to settle for getting out of trouble first, and getting as much distance as you can second.

Most of the time, however, you can hit out of a fairway bunker about as far as from the fairway, although the shot is a lot tougher to set up. You have to dig your feet in—I usually wiggle my feet until I feel I'm on solid footing—and then start your swing.

The important thing about hitting out of a fairway bunker is to catch the ball first. If you make an error on the fairway and

hit behind the ball, you may still get fairly good results, but not from sand.

When you hit behind the ball in a bunker, the ball comes out "soft," and you only get about two-thirds the distance you had expected. If you are going to make an error in a trap, you want to take the ball "thin"—that is, with only a small amount of sand.

As it turns out, that fairway bunker never figures into my game, nor does the water hazard. The latter is about 300 yards away, and so is beyond any tee shot I might hit.

What is required, however, is an accurate tee shot. The twelfth at Olympia Fields is another dogleg right, about 390 yards long, and a difficult driving hole. The trees on both sides demand a drive pretty much down the middle of the fairway. I seem to drive better on holes where there is trouble on both sides rather than on one side only. I probably concentrate just a tad more than usual, and perhaps subconsciously strive more for accuracy when I'm under pressure.

In any event, I aim right down the middle, and that is where the ball goes. Once you accomplish a good drive on this hole, the rest is fairly routine.

Now it is time for a par-3. The thirteenth at Olympia Fields is a rare hole. It has a blind green. The tee is elevated but you cannot see the surface of the green because it is obscured by the two bunkers in front of the green.

I ask the club members in our foursome where the pin is, and they think it is in the middle of the green, but nobody is sure.

I take a chance and aim for the middle of the green. If in doubt, that's a pretty good rule to follow.

It turns out that the pin is a little bit farther back than the center of the green, but my 7-iron shot is unusually good and the ball lands just about three feet from the cup, giving me an easy birdie.

There was an element of luck in my shot. The wind was blowing from right to left, which made it an easier shot. I was able to aim for the center of the green and let the wind do the

work of carrying my ball toward the cup. This is another example of how the wind can influence your shot—in this case, favorably.

There is one other thing about the thirteenth hole at Olympia that I should mention. There is water on the left of the green, but for the confident player it doesn't constitute a problem. He can block it out of his thinking because he is confident his tee shot will be adequate to reach the green.

You can do the same!

The great hole at Olympia Fields' north course is the fourteenth. It is deservedly one of the classic golf holes anywhere in the world.

You tee off from an elevated location. Just ahead is impossible rough. Along the right fairway is a creek that, farther down, cuts across the fairway. There are trees on either side that give you little chance to escape if you land in them. The final challenge is an elevated and blind green.

There are many ways to go wrong on this hole, and most golfers who play it regularly find them. If you stray too far left or right, you can wind up in trouble. If you shoot short, you face the creek and, beyond it, an uphill thicket of heavy rough.

The way to conquer the fourteenth is to hit a good drive down the fairway and just short of the creek. This positions you for a shot to the green; but that shot involves some special problems that you may also encounter on other courses.

When you are shooting for an elevated target, it is easy to be deceived. It looks a lot farther away than it really is, and you have to be careful not to overclub your shot.

My tee shot is well nigh perfect, landing just about at the marker showing that I have 150 yards left to reach the green. Because the shot is downwind, my choice between a 7-iron and an 8-iron is marginal. The difference is the location of the pin.

Today the pin is near the rear of the green, and so I add another five yards on my distance estimate. My "safe" choice was the 8-iron. It would have gotten me onto the green without difficulty.

At this point in my planning I become greedy. I figure that if I hit a 7-iron I can get even closer to the cup and consequently have an easier time making my birdie.

Unfortunately, it turns out to be too much club, and I wind up making the mistake I have constantly been warning you about: The ball goes over the green, giving me an almost automatic bogey.

You can summarize the fourteenth at Olympia very simply. It contains all kinds of trouble, and the only way to really play it is with a series of good shots. And I didn't.

Hole number fifteen provides still another golf lesson. It is a tough par-5, and today is playing even tougher because we're shooting into the wind. I encounter a problem I didn't anticipate.

I hit a tee shot that doesn't feel bad. As a matter of fact, the swing feels pretty good, but obviously something is wrong because I drove the ball into the water hazard on the right. I suspect I didn't stay with my shot long enough, or that I hit too far inside the line.

Whatever caused it, my drive on the fifteenth turns out to be the most disastrous shot of my round and costs me a penalty stroke. Because it is a lateral hazard—the water runs alongside the fairway—I do not have to shoot over again from the tee. Instead, I am able to drop the ball and take my third shot from a spot where the drive headed into the water.

At this point there is a real danger of my getting mad about flubbing a shot into the water. It is natural. Here we are, moving along at a pretty good pace, and suddenly I hit a dumb shot.

This is the time to apply the axiom that you must hit one shot at a time. It is too late to undo the shot that went into the water. That's past. Now we have to pick up the challenge anew.

Besides making you get mad and destroying your concentration, a bad shot may tempt you to make up for lost ground.

Fortunately, over the years I have pretty much learned to keep myself under control by reminding myself that there is no

way to reach the green from where a particular shot lies, and letting the matter go.

Moreover, the place to make up for a lost shot—if you can—isn't your penalty shot from the fairway but on the next one: your approach shot to the green. The key is to do this by hitting a good position shot.

That's what I do now. I hit my third shot where I want it to go; it lands in the fairway about 130 yards from the green, and I have a good lie.

Now I face a choice between a hard 9-iron and a soft 8-iron shot, and I choose the 8-iron. But I don't get enough distance on my approach shot; the ball lands short of the pin and I wind up with a bogey. Had I hit the ball better, I might have been able to putt for a par-5 despite my poor tee shot and water penalty.

Under the circumstances, a bogie wasn't a bad score. But now a new and potentially dangerous situation is developing. Although I have generally been playing well all day, I have now had two bogeys in a row.

That changes the momentum of my game.

Now there is a glimmer of doubt creeping into my thinking.

When you're hitting the ball well, your confidence runs high. If you're hitting it close to the pin, you start to think you can't hit it any other place. You have faith in yourself and your game and it shows.

But when you make a few errors, you can run into the danger of starting to doubt your own game, and that spells trouble. You can't second-guess yourself and you can't let uncertainty creep into your golf thinking without inviting real trouble.

The best cure for my problem is to hit a great tee shot on the sixteenth hole and start to roll again. But that isn't to be.

The sixteenth hole is one of those par-3s at Olympia Fields, all downhill.

Today they are repairing the tees. Instead of the 160-yard tee shot that we normally use, we drive from the front tees which are about 130 yards from the green. My iron shot lands short and spins about a foot back off the green.

This leaves me about a twenty-foot chip shot for a birdie, and I really try for it. But it doesn't drop and I have to settle for a putt and a par. A birdie would have been better, of course, but at least I broke the string of bogeys.

My chip shot involved another question—whether to leave the flag in or out of the hole. Since I was off the green, I had that option.

The rule that I follow is to always leave the pin in the cup if I'm chipping downhill and to take it out on an uphill chip shot.

There is a very important reason for this. If the pin is on the downslope, the flag leans back in the hole, giving you a bigger target; on the upslope, it tilts forward and limits your access to the hole.

Where the conditions are favorable for leaving the flag in the cup, it is an advantage because the pin will stop a ball that is too strong—and often give you a good bounce into the cup as well.

I use the same rule for leaving the pin in or out of the cup when I'm approaching the green or trying a putt from off the green. On the green, of course, the rules require you to take the pin out.

We are now coming to the seventeenth hole and my next to last chance to tilt the odds in my favor. This time I have a choice off the tee. I can drive for distance if I want to, but the seventeenth is only a 360-yard hole and I don't think there is any great advantage in the extra yardage.

Instead I opt for a 3-wood because the fairway is much wider at the point where the ball will land than the spot, farther on, where a driver would have carried.

It boils down to this—I lose a little distance off the tee but gain a better opportunity for my follow-up shot because I have a good fairway lie about 135 yards from the cup.

At this point the wind is behind me, and I hit an excellent 9-iron shot about ten feet past the cup. I then make the putt for a one-under-par 3.

Now we're on the final tee.

There is always a temptation to go all out on the eighteenth hole. A great many golfers, particularly inexperienced ones, adopt an all-or-nothing gambling attitude when they get to that last tee. They think it is a chance, the last chance, to pick up some lost strokes.

Not only does the golf gambler think he can ''get well'' if he can put together a series of spectacular shots, but there is an additional lure. On many courses the eighteenth is a long and difficult par-4, and that creates an urge to let out the shaft and strive for extra yardage.

Actually we should be smarter than that. The Packards have already warned us that the final hole is probably going to be the toughest of the eighteen holes on a golf course. The architect wants to wind up the course with a flourish, and he's not about to give you anything easy to shoot at.

And we also know that wishful thinking rarely pays off. On the contrary, getting reckless on the eighteenth hole is often the cause of a good score ballooning upward. I know because I have been guilty of it, and today is one of those times.

I'm hitting into the wind and trying to hit a hard shot but still seeking to keep it low. I try for some extra power, and don't shift my weight fast enough to my left side.

This lets the clubhead get ahead of the shaft, and naturally it turns as I hit the ball. The ball pulls about 30 yards into the left rough. This is certainly no place to wind up if you're trying to get a decent score.

However, I am lucky. There are a lot of trees in the area where my ball lands, and they can effectively block shots back into the fairway. But I wind up on the cart path and have a visible shot to the fairway.

My objective is obvious. Having driven into the rough, I need to get back onto the fairway with my second shot. I don't want to fall into the error that Oscar Miles described—hitting two bad shots in a row.

The correct thing to do is to hit a good shot out into the fairway. I will then be within a wedge shot of the green for my

third shot; follow up with two putts, and have my par on eighteen.

Instead, I break Oscar Miles' rule and hit another bad shot. Not only don't I get the ball back on the fairway, I leave it in the rough. Not only is it in the rough, it is in the WRONG rough!

Because the pin is on the left side of the green and my ball is in the left rough, there is no way I can put my ball close to the cup. I do the next best thing, and aim for the center of the green.

I hit my target and have a thirty foot putt, which I play too boldly. It overshoots the cup by five feet, but I make the second putt coming back. This gives me a par—a drive, a flubbed second shot, an approach, and two putts—but it comes the hard way.

Going back over the hole, you can see that if I had hit either a decent drive or a good second shot, I would have had the right distance for a wedge to take me into range for a makeable birdie putt. Instead my errors forced me to scramble to avoid a bogey.

On the scorecard, it wasn't a bad day. I had a 70, one stroke under par for the eighteen holes: three birdies and two bogeys; but as we saw, I didn't play well on the final holes and was fortunate that my earlier play saved the day for me. My partner had an 82; our opponents shot a 79 and an 80.

Chapter 11

Correcting Your Mistakes

What can you learn from the round of golf I have just described? The first thing is that it was far from a perfect eighteen holes. My shots off the tee were below average. I had one penalty shot, one drive that almost went out of bounds, and more than half my tee shots were in the rough.

By rights that should have sabotaged my score, yet I wound up with a respectable 70. Why? Because in most instances, even when the ball wasn't in the fairway, it was just a few feet off course. Except on the fifteenth and eighteenth holes, my tee shot—good or not—was generally in the correct pathway to the green.

Moreover, I made up for most of my errors off the tee with reasonably effective approach shots and—what is vital to par golf—I never had to do more than two-putt a green.

Had I played better on the back nine, I could have put my score down into the 60s, which is where champions are made. As it was, however, I had some favorable breaks that probably saved me a stroke or two.

What about your game? How would you have fared on these same eighteen holes at Olympia Fields? Until you actually play the course, you will never know. However, there are several generalities I have noted that apply to most golfers.

The first of these are three common errors made by players who score in the 80s.

1. Faulty strategy.
2. Errors that are made fairly consistently.
3. A lack of consistency through the entire round and, more than likely, "blowing up" on a few holes.

By a coincidence, our foursome fit those categories. See if you can spot your prototype.

One of the players failed to play par golf primarily because he hadn't mastered position golf. His drives covered good distances, but he consistently wound up in the wrong part of the fairway. This meant that even though he got yardage off the tee, he was setting the stage for errors with his fairway irons and in his approach shots. On almost every hole he was being forced to shoot from the wrong angle to the green.

Even though this golfer had very good mechanical skills, there was no way he could buck the odds all day long without paying a price in extra strokes.

My partner played better position golf, but lacked consistency. He played about nine of his shots poorly, and these were the strokes over par that put him up to the 80-mark.

The fourth player also played about nine shots poorly, but he confined his errors to just a few holes. He seemed to make one error and then compound it with still another, and occasionally even a third. This was like the gambler at the poker table who sends good money after bad.

These are all mental or strategy errors; now let's see how we can spot some of these errors in our own game, and equally important, seek out the remedies.

If you are golfer who finds yourself almost, but not quite, down into a scratch game, I suggest that you sit down with your scorecard and replay your last round. The card will give you the first hint. Look for any double bogeys. If you had any, why did they happen?

Next, take a look at the holes where you scored a bogey. If they were early holes, there is a good chance you were neglecting your warmup. A drive that is pushed or off line is usually traceable to the failure to be properly loosened up.

If you were drawing a poor line on the green or if there was improper speed on your putts, it is likely you didn't spend time on the practice green and were "guessing" during the early holes.

If you spot a series of bogeys, your scorecard may tell you something else. You may recall that I experienced this in the closing holes of my round.

A string of poor scores may stem from a letdown in your concentration; more frequently, it begins with one error that undermines your self confidence, and thereby multiplies into a series of errors.

In my experience, you can usually spot what is wrong by looking at your mistakes. Looking for trouble where you found it is a perfectly logical notion.

But not always. There are times when your troubles are masked behind some of those par and even birdie holes. The golfer in our foursome who was making errors on his iron shots actually did this by improper placement of his tee shots.

One way to determine if there is a "hidden" fault in your game is to carefully examine your unexpectedly good shots. Check carefully to find out whether they were really the result of good technique or came from just plain luck.

It is also a good idea to reexamine your golf thinking from time to time. If you play the same course fairly consistently, keep you scorecards and compare them. You may be able to detect which holes tend to give you the most trouble.

Go one step further and study your scores shot-by-shot, and you may be able to deduce which phase of your game needs work. Are you playing each hole in the most effective manner? Are you consistently approaching the green from the best angle? If not, why not?

It is even worthwhile to find out if you are unconsciously settling into a comfortable pattern of play—such as using a 7-iron on a given par-3 hole by habit.

If the 7-iron normally gets you on or near the green, it is probably the right club. But it also may not be. Perhaps an easy 6-iron shot will give you extra accuracy. You can track down

many of the reasons for the extra strokes you are taking during a round. But if those "lost strokes" are caused by poor golf technique, my best advice is to consult a golf pro. He is trained to spot errors in swing, hand position, and choice of club.

The other errors—poor planning, poor strategy, or a poor mental approach to the game—the golfer himself can correct. As a matter of fact, he is probably the only one who can.

We've talked about the 80-shooter, but what about the 90-plus golfer. What kind of errors does he make, and how can they be spotted?

The higher handicap player quite obviously has a higher score because he makes more errors. It is as simple as that. What isn't so simple is to identify his flaws, because the golfer with scores in this range tends to be inconsistent.

The starting point, just as with the lower scoring player, is the scorecard, to see whether there are certain holes that seem to cause trouble.

With that thought in mind, let's go back to Olympia Fields. This time I want you to plan how *you* should play some of the key holes on the course. By doing this you can pick up some pointers on how to play holes with similar characteristics on your home course. It will also give you some insight into a course you're playing for the first time.

There will also be differences between Olympia Fields and your course, and it is important to understand them.

Before you tee off on any new course you must establish some guidelines. You must determine your basic golf skills. Your usual score provides the basic yardstick.

It is important, however, to be candid in establishing this. On your home course you have an established record. You know just about what you are going to score on a given day, and what the cause of a higher or lower score may be on any particular day.

If, on the other hand, you are playing a strange course, you have to "adjust" your score. One factor that can affect your score is where you have been playing your golf.

How much better—or worse—you do on a new course will

depend to a great extent on its length and, more importantly, on the difficulty of the rough.

If you have been playing a public course with wide-open fairways, you will have to add strokes if and when you play a private course. You will land in the rough more often, and it will be tougher rough than you have been used to.

By contrast, if you are going from a tough course to an easier one, you may count on doing better.

Nevertheless, a strange course, even if technically easier than your own, is likely to add strokes to your game simply because you aren't familiar with the terrain. A course with very fast greens will add strokes to even the best golfer's game.

Take all these factors into consideration in determining what your "true" handicap is.

The next step is to decide which golfer profile best describes your current game.

In my experience, there are five categories of golfer:

1. The top amateur. On his best days, this golfer will have scores very close to par. On an exceptional round, he will turn in a sub-par score. Depending upon his putting skill he will usually average somewhere in the 70s, and on a rare off-day will go up into the low 80s. Most clubs will not have many top amateurs beyond the club champion and his immediate challengers.

2. The "first class" amateur. This player is a good competitor. He will average in the low 80s. On a bad round he may go as high as 90 and on a good round down into the 70s. His ambition is to shoot par. He's come close, but never quite made it.

3. The "good" amateur. This golfer will average right around 90. When things break his way, his score goes down into the mid-80s; a really bad day will hurt his pride and his score, and he may not break 100. On most days, however, this golfer is comfortable on any golf course, and can play competitively in most foursomes.

4. "Mr. Average" is the golfer who has to fight to break

100, and when he does, it is a red-letter day. He comes in all sizes, shapes, and ages, but he has one outstanding characteristic: the dream of getting his game consistently below 100.

5. The fifth group covers everybody else, from the neophyte on the first hole of his first round of golf to the veteran player who is still struggling to overcome some basic problems in his game that makes him a consistent 100-plus player.

In thinking about your golf game, the place to start is with the par-3 holes.

For the moment, I am going to confine my remarks to the ''short'' par-3s—the ones that run about 150 yards in length.

These are the great equalizers. Every golfer has a better chance here to match any other golfer than he will on the driving holes, because he can reach the green on all but the longest of the par-3s.

There are many times on the golf course when a high-handicap player must think cautiously; but not on a par-3 hole. I don't think you should play a short par-3 any differently whether you are still trying to break 100 or whether you're the club champion.

This is the place to go all out. It is one of those opportunities to shoot for par, and you shouldn't pass it by.

You begin by aiming for the green, for a simple reason: If you land your tee shot on the green, it is a lot easier to sink the ball in two putts and get your par. What you want to avoid is not getting the ball on the green. Missing the green makes it tougher to get down in two srokes.

Take time to review your scorecards and you'll find that you most often make your par 3 on those holes where you get the ball on the green or, at worst, in the fringe just off the green.

Your scores go up when the ball fails to reach the green and goes off line into the rough or falls into one of the sand traps that usually guard the green on a par-3. Clearly then, the most important shot on a par-3 hole is the tee shot.

This is a good place to review some of the points we discussed earlier in the book. The first step toward a good tee shot

is to tee up the ball. That gives you the best possible lie for your ball.

If on a given hole your companions tee off first and you have a good idea of the distance they should get with a given club, you can sometimes double-check your estimate of the wind factor.

Otherwise your tee shot is a matter between you, the ball, your club, and your strategy for playing the hole, and to the extent that you can, you should block out everything else.

The next reminder is to select the correct club. Ignore your golfing companions. You are hitting your golf ball; they aren't.

Your club selection should depend on the characteristics of the hole and the distance from the tee to the cup. This is where the better player differs from the beginner.

The beginner lets the yardage marker dictate his choice of club. The better player chooses his club by seeing the shot in his mind and deciding which club will carry the right distance.

For example, I rarely say to myself that I am going to hit a ball 150 yards. Instead, I think of it in terms of club-distance. In my case, on a day without wind, I hit a 7-iron 150 yards. Thus, I have learned to judge 150 yards not in yards, but as a 7-iron shot.

Obviously, this requires that you know your distances.

The place to start is at 150 yards. This is almost a benchmark in golf—150 yards from a given tree to the green; 150 yards from a bush; 150 yards from tee to green.

If you keep watching and learning on the golf course, you will very quickly be able to identify just how far 150 yards is from where you are standing. Judging other distances is then a simple matter of basic arithmetic: 160 yards is 10 yards farther, 140 yards is 10 yards nearer, and so forth.

A pro will probably hit a 7-iron or an 8-iron for a 150-yard shot; a pretty good golfer will hit a 6-iron; and a shorter hitter will probably use a 5-iron. But these numbers mean nothing. Which of your clubs will give *you* a 150-yard shot?

Most golfers' distances will vary ten yards between clubs.

Therefore, if you hit a 6-iron 150 yards, you will need a 5-iron to carry 160 yards and will have to drop down to a 7-iron for a 140-yard shot.

The 10-yard difference is simply an estimate; it is important that you know your own game well enough to judge how much farther the ball goes when you drop down one club, and how much distance you take off your shot by switching to a more lofted club.

In making these estimates, you also have to allow for the wind. You may recall that earlier in the book we estimated that every mile per hour of headwind will cut your distance a yard and a half, while a following wind of the same speed will add that amount of distance.

In general, a gentle headwind will probably require your using a club one number lower than you would ordinarily use (a 5-iron instead of a 6-iron), and a moderately strong wind may require going two clubs down (a 4-iron instead of a 6-iron). Obviously the choice is reversed if you are hitting with the wind to your back.

There is another major consideration. You usually have to take a little more club if you are shooting to an elevated green; you can take a little less club if the green is below you.

One other thing: I have warned you many times about the dangers of overshooting the green on any hole because it almost always leaves you with a tough downhill chip shot. Higher handicap players may want to break this rule on par-3 holes.

Most golfers who shoot in the 90s and higher have a tendency to underestimate par-3s and shoot short. Frequently this puts them into deep trouble, because the front and sides of the short par-3s are usually the most heavily trapped areas.

In this case you may find it to your advantage to take a chance on shooting long rather than landing short.

As we've said, the route to par golf on the par-3s is clearly to get your tee shot on the green. But that doesn't always happen. What then? Your next priority is the same as it is anywhere on the golf course—get your next shot in play.

Simply stated, this means that if you fail to get on the green on a par-3 hole with your tee shot, you must get on the green with your second shot.

Ideally, of course, your recovery shot will put you close enough to the cup to still make your par, but that should be a secondary consideration. Your first goal is to get on the putting green so that you at least preserve a bogey.

Let's take a par-3 hole from the tee. You can pick the routine that suits you best, but in my case, here's how I play such a hole.

Before I walk onto the tee, I pick the club I think is the right one. Then I walk to the teeing area and inspect the hole. This means evaluating the traps and problem areas and selecting my target area.

Next I choose the best spot to tee up the ball. If there is trouble, I follow the standard rule of teeing up on the side of trouble. Finally I check the distance and the wind factor.

Now I have all the input I need, and it is time for a final decision. Have I chosen the right club? At this point I have to make a firm decision and stick to it.

I know you've had this experience, everybody has: You pick a 6-iron, for example, but then think it may leave you short. What do you do? You either hurry your swing or try to compensate by swinging harder, and you destroy your rhythm.

If you have doubts about your club selection, you will probably try to correct them in the tempo of your swing.

The golfer who thinks he has picked too weak a club will try to hit harder; the golfer who thinks at the last moment that he has too much club is likely to second-guess himself and, just before impact, decelerate his swing—an almost certain way to flub a shot.

The remedy is obvious. Pick the club that you think will do the job. Double-check your decision as you size up the hole. If you have doubts, step back and ponder some more.

But once you step up to the ball, do so with confidence in your decision and hit the ball with conviction that you are right.

* * *

Olympia Fields has four par-3s—numbers six, eight, thirteen, and sixteen. Three of them come within our definition of "makeable" par-3s. The scorecard distance on the sixth and thirteenth holes is just over 140 yards from the regular tees and about 155 from the championship tees.

For most players, these two holes demand a typical 150-yard tee shot. The sixteenth hole is just slightly longer. During the round I described earlier in this book, this hole was under repair. It normally plays about 157 yards from the regular tee and 170 from the back tees.

We have already established that every player, regardless of scoring ability, should aim to put his tee shot in the middle of the green. The key to doing this is to translate the tee-to-green distance into the club you believe will let you put your ball on the green.

This is the club-distance element I spoke about earlier, and as you noticed when I played those holes, I determine it not only from the scorecard distance, but also from the placement of the pin and the strength and direction of the wind.

Par on a 150-yard hole can be made in two ways—a tee shot to the green and two putts, or a tee shot off the green followed by a chip shot and a single putt.

The par golfer can use this as one yardstick in adjusting to longer holes. A par-4 hole requires a drive to within 150 yards of the green followed by 3 strokes to sink the ball. A par-5 hole gives him two strokes to get within the 150-yard range.

Let's translate that into distances. A scratch golfer should set the goal of consistently shooting par-3s on holes up to 150 yards long; of making par on par-4 holes up to 380 yards long; and of regularly shooting par-5s on holes up to 600 yards long.

It is the longer holes that can add strokes to his game. The fourth of the par-3s at Olympia Fields, for example, is over 200 yards long. This is one place where a golfer may lose a stroke to par.

There are no par-5s at Olympia Fields that run over 600 yards, but six of the par-4s are over 400 yards in length, and

these become a special challenge to any golfer seeking to shoot par or better.

Obviously, not all par golfers shoot consistent par golf on every hole. Instead they aim for par and try to balance any hole where they go one-over with a birdie on a subsequent hole. They also try to avoid making double-bogeys because it is hard to pick up two strokes.

You can make a birdie on any hole, of course. But it is usually on the shorter par-4s and par-5s that pro golfers get their birdies, and these are usually traceable to a super second-shot which either reaches the green, or a "friendly" lie off the green with a clear shot at the pin.

Another way a pro gets birdies—and sometimes enough of them to turn in a sub-par round—is by getting hot in and around the greens. He can pick up strokes on the putting green—sometimes with a chip shot that holes out—or, more often, with lag putts that hit the cup squarely and drop in.

And what happens when the pro shoots over par? Those are the days when the putts don't fall or—particularly on the longer holes—when percentages catch up with him.

The par I have just described is for the scratch player, and can apply to the golfer who scores in the 70s or low 80s. These players can and should tackle each hole with the view of scoring par and, where possible, making a birdie.

If you are a low-handicap player, I believe you have to play aggressively whenever you have the chance. However, that doesn't mean playing recklessly or blithely ignoring dangers.

Even a Tom Watson will put his driver in the bag and pull out a 1-iron on some tees—not to play safe, but to increase his odds by putting greater emphasis on his second shot. What this means is that the better player has to attack the course, and not play defensively, if he is to score well.

I put the golfer who shoots in the low 80s in that same group. If that describes your game, I think you too should shoot for par on every hole, but should add one other factor: Make every effort to avoid shooting double-bogeys on any hole. And as Oscar Miles observed, double bogeys are usually trace-

able to making a bad shot and then following it with a second one.

If the 80-shooter avoids double-bogeys, he can shoot his usual score if he bogeys half the holes and makes par on the rest. And if he can make par on ten or more of the holes, he can bring his score down into the 70s.

On the other hand, I believe that any golfer who shoots in the 90s and above has to take a different point of view.

Everybody can dream about shooting a par-71 course in even-par, but that simply isn't going to happen to the player who normally shoots in the 90s and above. All the breaks and all the luck in the world won't reduce his score that much.

The higher handicap golfer can't reasonably expect to shoot par golf when he gets to the longer holes. It is pointless for him to check out his scorecard against par, since for him par is—or can be—totally misleading.

Ordinarily, the standards for par are considered to be two putts per green, with the remaining strokes allotted to reaching the green.

But that is not the way golf is actually played. Even the best players in the world would have trouble breaking par if they consistently used two putts per green, and any good player who has had to use all thirty-six putts in a round of golf has either had an off-day with his putter or has consistently reached the greens with his irons but left himself very long approach putts.

If you are a higher handicap player, I suggest you change your thinking about par right now.

The golfer who shoots 90 or above should practice what I call "Handicap Par." By this I mean a system of par figures that actually match your game.

Handicap Par is simple. You simply add an extra stroke to the par figures on the scorecard. Thus, all par-3s over 150 yards become par-4s, par-4s become par-5s, and par-5s become par-6s.

This may be just a gimmick, but it works.

Take the eighth hole at Olympia Fields, which measures over 200 yards long. On the scorecard, it is a par-3; but if you

apply Handicap Par, you have two strokes to reach the green. Follow up with two putts and you have a realistic four strokes to achieve your par.

The first hole at Olympia is another example of where to use Handicap Par. Its regular tees are 485 yards from the green, and the championship tees more than 500 yards away. The par golfer usually feels he has to get a good drive—something like 250 yards—to give himself a decent second shot to the green and then, depending on his putting, to score a par or a birdie.

If you are a 90-plus shooter and try the same strategy, you may pull it off every once in a while. But if you examine your record, I think you will find that swinging so hard that it throws you off balance often starts a string of trouble—an off-line drive into the rough, a muffed recovery—and still leaves you a couple of hundred yards from paydirt and only two strokes to make par.

Suppose, on the other hand, you recognize that your personal par is not a 5 but a 6. Using this Handicap Par, you have a much more realistic goal to shoot for.

On a par-4 hole your personal par is not a 4 but a 5. Now you have not just one but two shots to get the ball within the 150-yard range. You can feel comfortable with a more modest shot off the tee, and a mid-iron shot will then put you well within the 150-yard marker.

What you have done is to concede the regular par-4 of the scratch golfer, but in exchange have gotten an excellent chance of getting a 5. Moreover, you have a chance at a bonus.

By setting more realistic goals for yourself, you take away a lot of pressure, and you can often pick up a stroke or two over the eighteen-hole route.

Chapter 12

Improving Your Chip Shots

So far, I have been encouraging you to think better golf. It is my belief that most golfers fail to improve because they continue to make errors in their golf thinking. They make the wrong judgment in decision-making situations. They can't or won't plan each shot properly before they take it.

As a result, even if they have a good swing and a sound grasp of golf mechanics, the best they can accomplish is a fair result. A well-stroked putt can be ruined if it is poorly aimed through faulty strategy or sloppy thinking about distance or slope.

A long, well-hit drive can prove illusory if it is aimed at the wrong part of the fairway. Well-executed iron shots can only make up part of the golf challenge if you are constantly thinking wrong and leaving yourself shots that fight the odds.

On the other hand, good strategy can go a long way toward getting a decent golf score even if the mechanics of your game aren't as polished as you would like them to be.

For this reason, if I had a choice between backing a player with good golf imagination but only fair ability and one with pretty good talent but no golf sense, I'd pick the one with the ability to think about his game. Most often, the smart golfer will win. This is also why I have encouraged you to work on your golf strategy first.

* * *

Now it's time to look at the mechanics of golf.

I think the toughest decision any golfer has to make is fundamental: How good a golfer does he want to be?

There is the quick answer: Any golfer wants to be a good as he can possibly be. A professional golfer can give that answer and, whether he likes it or not, he can be pretty realistic about his game.

He doesn't have much room for guesswork. First, he must qualify to be a professional, and then he must maintain a given standard to stay on the tour. He has to meet a strict standard of tournament play, and make an income from his winnings, or retire.

There are other yardsticks for the pro. He has to play well enough to make a living at golf. I did that myself for quite a few years, and even when I dropped out of the tour was still making the grade financially.

There are also some players who qualify as "journeymen." They play well enough to afford to be able to keep going. Most often you find their names somewhere down in the list of also-rans. Obviously they want to be better golfers. They'd like to hit the jackpot, if only once in a while. But the odds are overwhelmingly against them, for a simple reason: Their game just isn't good enough.

It is a lot more difficult for the nonprofessional to be realistic about his game. He may always hope that he'll find an overnight cure for his golfing woes, and that his score will shrink, but even the most optimistic golfer eventually learns that wishful thinking doesn't cure an erratic golf game. It takes hard work and determination. What really counts is how much time and effort you can afford to spend on your game.

The occasional golfer has limits to how well he can score. It is well nigh impossible to gain consistency if you can play only once a week, or not even that often.

There is another important factor in becoming a better golfer. You must ask yourself how much you really want to change your game. In my opinion, a great majority of golfers

are probably better off working on their present game than trying to build a new one. You take a lot of the fun out of golf when you get too serious about your score.

The best way for most golfers to improve is to take their present game and polish it up. If you have followed the advice I've given in the earlier pages of this book, you are showing improvement. You are no longer making the mistakes that formerly cost you strokes every time you went out to play golf.

Once you have stopped making errors in judgment and have gotten rid of the bad golf habits that crept into your game, you can still progress. Nobody can ever take too much time working on their golf confidence, and the confident golfer is going to consistently shoot better golf.

If that isn't enough—if you want to shoot still better golf— you will have to face up to hard realities. Very probably, your game has mechanical deficiencies. You simply don't strike the ball correctly or, if you do, you do not consistently make proper contact. That's a lot tougher problem to solve.

There are many reasons for this problem. One of them is the golfer's attitude. Let me illustrate this. At my golf club there are two golfers who have about a 27 handicap. They share many of the problems of the high-handicap player. Perhaps you'll find some of your own in their experience.

One of these golfers is not very husky. He doesn't have the strength to hit the ball with any power. For that reason he has to make the most of his abilities. He has to play accurate golf if he is to keep pace with the longer hitters. Unfortunately, this player isn't going to develop accuracy and won't get any better even though he puts in a lot more playing time than most golfers. His trouble? He constantly gets himself involved in golf mechanics. He has taken lessons all over the world. He takes a trip for a week to this teacher, then he goes to another teacher.

All of this has only made him more confused today than ever. Yet this is a common problem for the 95 to 100 golfer. Most of them get caught up in the hotbed of mechanics. They read a lot of golf articles and they take a little from each.

They have the illusion that a good golfer makes a good

teacher, which is simply not true. Nor does it necessarily follow that a good teacher is a good golfer. The real challenge to a golf teacher is whether he can translate his game into yours.

I believe that you must tailor your game to yourself. The role of the good teacher isn't to try to turn you into a carbon copy of himself. What a good golf teacher does, in my opinion, is to help you cut down your margin of error. He takes your game—as it is—and tries to spot the places where you can make adjustments and increase your chances of success. And that's what I'm going to try to do.

I've already described the golfer who is suffering from too much advice. All things considered, he's a pretty good player. He plays to his handicap a lot better than the second golfer I mentioned above.

This second golfer has no reason not to be a good one. He has the desire and the strength and he is a younger player. Moreover, he has played golf for only four or five years, and so shouldn't have deeply ingrained golfing habits. But he does. For one thing, he is stubborn. For example, in taking a short pitch shot to the green, he should concentrate on getting the ball onto the green and then letting it roll toward the cup. Instead he consistently tries to pitch the ball all the way to the hole.

He makes this kind of error in judgment too often. He hits a lot of mechanically good shots, but simply doesn't have good golf imagination and will probably never reach his potential. These two golfers typify the two basic problem golfers—the one who has the mechanics but has trouble with his imagination; the other who may hit five shots, all of them different.

Fortunately there is an approach that works for both kinds of golfers—provided, of course, that they want to improve their game. And that is a big proviso. As I pointed out earlier, just about everyone thinks he would like to play better, but that's not enough. You have to be willing to work at it.

Right off the bat, the golfer who wants to improve the mechanics of his game must make a commitment: He must give

up the idea of any short-term cure, and must be willing to get worse before he can get better.

This is so important that I will repeat it.

In order to get better, a golfer must first be willing to get worse.

There are many reasons why learning to play golf well isn't an easy task. First, there are relatively few "natural" golfers. I didn't take up golf myself until I was fifteen. At the time I was involved with baseball.

My father was an enthusiastic golfer and a member of the Tam O'Shanter Club. But I didn't pay much attention until my brother, who was an avid golfer, brought some of his friends home from the University of Houston and I shagged balls for him.

I took lessons from Johnny Revolta when I was in high school. Johnny, even then, was a golfing legend. Back in the 1930s he won the PGA, the Western Open, and many other name tournaments. Later, as the pro at Evanston Golf Club, he became one of the great teachers of golf. He was my first teacher and probably the most knowledgeable pro I ever met.

His greatest contribution to my game—and to dozens of professionals and amateurs who were his students—was his emphasis on developing a good short game.

As a matter of fact, it is my belief that good golf is built on an ability to master the chip shot. If you can do that, you have the cornerstone of a sound golf game. Conversely, if you look at the problems of most golfers, you find they have not mastered the short game.

Take my fellow club member who suffers from taking too many golf lessons. He thinks he has a good short game, but doesn't. It isn't bad. It is one reason he shoots his handicap, and occasionally turns in a round of 80, which is about a stroke per hole better than his average. But it should be better. He simply has never learned consistent technique. The same is true for the other golfer—the one with natural talent but a poor golf imagination.

He really doesn't know what the ball is supposed to do when

he hits it, even if he hits it correctly. He has never really had to learn how to hit a golf ball, and so has never bothered to think about it. As a consequence, his mental attitude and physical ability are rarely in synch.

There is a third basic type of high-handicap player—the late starter. He didn't take up golf until he was an adult, and maybe even well along in years. That is one of the great things about golf: It really has no age barrier. It is one of the true lifetime sports.

Ideally, however, I think a golfer should learn the game as a youngster. That is why I encourage my friends to have their children learn the game as early as possible. Youngsters are likely to have a natural rhythm and sense of balance and, if they learn the basics correctly, will have the foundation for a consistent swing that will stay with them through the years.

The adult beginner isn't likely to be as rhythmic, as coordinated, or as athletic as the younger player. This doesn't mean that he can't become a good golfer; but it does mean that he has to learn some parts of the game that the youngster picks up almost intuitively.

I could continue to put golfers into various categories, but one final one will do for now: The golfer who has been playing golf long enough to have built-in problems. The chronic slicer is probably the most common of these. He hits the ball erratically on short shots, and with his long irons and woods sends it into a long curving arc to the right—the classic slice.

There are golfers who can "control" their slice. They know that the ball is going to curve to the right and so deliberately aim left, confident that the ball will come back around. They are like the old-time riflemen who allowed for "windage" when they aimed at their target.

But most slicers are not consistent. The ball slices, all right, but rarely does it slice the same way two times in succession. Sometimes it pushes out to the left, sometimes it goes straight ahead before curving, and sometimes it zooms out to the right and keeps right on going.

Earlier I suggested that many golfers are better off settling

for their present game and then working on lowering their score by concentrating on their golf strategy. The slicer is the one exception to this. He has to get rid of his slice before he can hope to have any control over his game.

Let's work on that right now.

There are innumerable stories of athletes with bulging muscles who have trouble hitting a golf ball 100 yards. Equally astonishing, to the uninitiated, is the ability of some deceptively small golfer who belts them out 250 yards or more.

Strength, by itself, is not essential to good golf. Clearly, it helps. Arnold Palmer has the arms of a blacksmith. But most of the top golfers are not conspicuously strong, except perhaps in the hands and wrists.

This is even more true among most amateurs. The 90-plus player is either physically strong but uncoordinated or, more likely, simply isn't highly athletic. Most high handicappers aren't going to boom out long drives or put fairway woods and irons into orbit.

What the good amateur can become, however, is *golf strong*. By this I mean an ability to hit the ball with force. This is particularly vital in hitting out of the rough. You must have control of the club and the ability to strike the ball decisively.

That comes from a sound grip, a comfortable stance, a confidence in your game, and the ability to practice effectively.

The place to start is with the short irons.

Every shot in golf is important, but you are on your way to mastering them all if you can master the chip shot. First, let me define the chip shot. It is a short shot from just off the green. The objective of the chip shot is simple—to get the ball into the air, have it land as quickly on the green as possible, and then have it roll toward the cup. You can use any short iron with which you feel most comfortable. Any club from a 5-iron through a 9-iron can qualify. Some golfers may find it best to stick with a single club.

There is an old rule in business: If something isn't broken, don't fix it. This same concept—don't tinker with success—

applies to chip shots. If you have one iron that puts the ball consistently where you want it to go on the green, stick to it.

Most golfers, however, adjust their selection of club to the specific circumstance they encounter in a round of golf. For example, I base my club selection for chip-shooting on these questions:

- How much green do I have to shoot for?
- What is the distance between the spot where my ball will land on the green and the pin?
- If it is a short distance to the cup, how much of a run can the ball make without overshooting?
- If the pin is set back, how far does the ball have to roll to reach the cup?
- What is the distance between the spot where my ball lies and the point where the green begins.

What I am looking for is a combination of two things—to get the ball onto the green and then to get it to roll to the cup. Essentially what I'm striving to do is get the ball on the green in such a way that it takes on the action of a well-stroked putt.

Let's break the chip shot into two parts. Our first objective is to get the ball onto the green. From close in we have a wide choice. We can reach the green with any of our shorter irons. Which do we choose? That depends on how much—or how little—roll you want after the ball lands. If there is plenty of green so that any short iron will provide the roll you want, the choice is easy: You'll want to use the one that will give you the maximum roll, on the theory that this is the closest you can come to imitating the action of a putt. Simply stated, if you have a choice of either the 5-iron or the 9-iron, pick the 5-iron.

Here is the rule: Use the least lofted club you can from your position. By loft I mean the angle at which the clubhead joins the shaft of the club. The greater the angle, the more lofted the club and the higher its number. (See Illustration #8.)

The reason for using the least lofted club in making a long-roll chip shot is to get the ball to the green as quickly as possi-

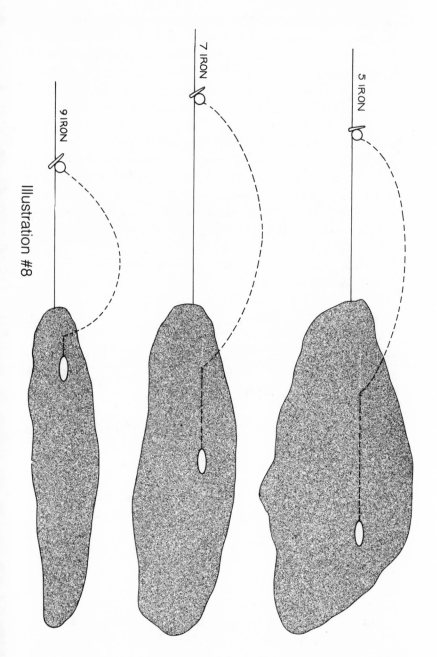

Illustration #8

ble, so that it will develop the maximum roll once it lands. In one common example of a chip shot, the ball is a few feet off the green. First I estimate the distance to the cup. Let's say it is about 12 feet.

Now I want to follow the rule of using the least lofted club to produce a ball that will roll the farthest distance. In this situation some golfers will chip with a 5-iron, or even a 2- or 3-iron, but I feel most comfortable using a 6-iron.

Next I have to decide where on the green I want the ball to land. There is a pretty good rule of thumb for a chip shot with the 6-iron: the ball should travel one-third of the way in the air and then roll the remaining two-thirds of the way to the cup.

This gives us a basis for our chip shot. We estimate the distance from the ball to the cup, pick a spot a third of the way there, aim for it, and let the rolling action of the ball do the rest. In this case the cup is twelve feet away, and I therefore want the ball to travel four feet in the air, land, and then roll the remaining eight feet to the cup.

What about other chip shots? It goes without saying that they are not always a 6-iron-shot away. Suppose you are shooting to a cup on the narrow side of the green and don't have enough room for a long roll. If you use a 6-iron, the the ball will land and then roll far past the cup. In this case we go to the second half of our formula: How much distance do we have between the spot where the ball will land and the cup?

If there is a little less running room than I need for a 6-iron, I'll opt for a 7-iron; if there is still less room I'll go to the 8-iron; and so forth. The deciding factor here is the amount of roll, and the more lofted the club, the more quickly the ball will stop. In an extreme case of minimum distance between the edge of the green and the pin, I'll use my most lofted club, the sand wedge.

To recap:

- Decide how far it is from where your ball lies to a spot safely on the green.

- Determine how much roll you will have to have between where your ball will land and where the cup is located.
- Pick the club that will "stop" the ball without over-running the cup.
- If you have a choice, pick the club with the least loft.

One way to picture a chip shot is to imagine that you're throwing a baseball at the cup. If you were looking for maximum accuracy, you wouldn't try to throw it at the cup with an overhand motion. Unless you were a pretty skilled player, that wouldn't work.

By contrast, a high toss might be all right. Thrown high, the ball would probably land, take a short bounce, and stop.

This approach requires great accuracy. To be successful you would have to judge quite precisely just how high to throw the ball and just how strong you would make the throw. That's hard to do consistently.

The third way of picturing the chip shot is the one that seems to work best for most people. To throw the ball as low as possible and then rely on its bounce and roll rather than try for the pinpoint accuracy of a high, arching throw.

The same factors apply in golf. You can attempt to pitch the ball onto the green as near the cup as possible, or you can try to run it up with a lower-flying shot in which it lands and runs. In general, the run-up shot is preferable, but that is not always possible. If, for example, you're confronted with a shot over a sand trap to a short green, you obviously have to try the high pitch to the green.

A good chip shot depends on good club selection. But it also depends on proper execution. You have to be able to hit the ball where you want it to go. The ball has to go far enough to reach the spot on the green that you have selected, and it has to be hit on the line you have picked out for reaching the cup. That means accuracy—and accuracy depends on grip, stance, and swing, the three basics of golf.

Let's talk first about grip.

Probably the first thing you heard when you took up golf

was about the "grip"—how you should hold the golf club. It is the subject of more golfing mumbo-jumbo than any other phase of the game and, I think, provides the biggest mental barrier to the average golfer.

If you stop and think about it, the club is simply an extension of your hands and arms, and your grip is therefore a direct contact between you and the ball. For this reason, a "poor grip" can be the source of a lot of golfing woe. In particular, a poor grip is the frequent cause of a slice.

But you can get into a lot worse trouble if you let yourself become too conscious of the grip. You can begin worrying about your grip and forget about concentrating on hitting the ball—and that would be real bad news. So let's forget all the technical business of gripping a golf club. Just pick up your 7-iron and let's go to work.

The first thing you want to do is pick the correct line between your ball and the cup. Put down a ball. Now place one of your golf clubs lengthwise on the ground in front of you. That club is going to represent the straight line between your ball and your target, the cup.

Position your clubhead behind the ball in doing this. There are three checkpoints. First, make sure the bottom of the clubhead is flat on the ground. Second, make sure the clubface is square to the target. Third, make sure the ball is in the middle of the clubface. Why are these three checkpoints important? Because they ensure that the clubface will strike the ball properly: Square to the target and on the "sweet spot"—the center of the clubface.

Next, let's grasp the shaft of the club. For the moment, start out with your regular grip on the 7-iron; now move your grip down three or four inches. That's about the correct place for your hands for a chip shot. You have moved your grip down on the club shaft to "tighten up" your swing and hence lessen your margin of error.

Now for your stance.

If you have gripped down on the club shaft and if you have kept the clubhead flat on the ground, you should be standing a

comfortable distance from the ball. You should be looking down at the ball and your arms should be be free to move naturally.

The most important thing in your stance is balance. On the chip shot, you want the clubhead to flow through the hitting area of your stroke. The best way to do that is to stand so that your body moves naturally through the swing.

I find that it helps to stand with my toes slightly turned out, my feet about six inches apart at the heels, and my left foot pulled just slightly back from the line to the cup. In other words, if I were to lay down a second golf club parallel to the first, but right at my feet, my right toe would be touching the club and my left toe would be about three inches back from the club.

I don't want you to take a tape measure and repeat my stance. It may or may not work for you. What you are seeking is a stance that feels comfortable and steady, with the ball at about the right distance from you and your clubhead resting squarely behind the ball.

The position of the ball is also a matter of personal preference, but most golfers find that it should either be on a line midway between your feet, or slightly to the right of center.

The chip shot consists of a simple motion. You start with the clubhead square to the ball. You take the clubhead back smoothly, keeping it consistently square to the ball. On the downswing you bring the clubhead back in the same plane so that it strikes the ball squarely in your original position.

Think about it. If you start out with the clubhead square to the ball and the clubhead never strays from the path that follows the line to the hole, and if you then return the clubhead in that path, the ball has to travel directly toward the hole. How you do that is primarily up to you in terms of grip, foot position, where you place the ball, and anything else involved in your shot.

Square . . . Takeaway . . . Square.

That's the formula for a good chip shot. Square to the ball.

Takeaway on the correct path. Return the clubhead squarely to the ball.

There are only two things that can go wrong. One is to take the clubhead outside the proper plane, either on the takeaway or on the downswing. That can result in a glancing blow that spins the ball off line. The second is to fail to bring the clubhead back squarely to the ball. This will also destroy your straight line to the cup.

A common reason for the second problem—failure to bring the clubhead back squarely to the ball—is a loose grip on the club at the instant of impact. Regardless of your style of grip, you must hold the shaft of the club firmly in your fingers so that it doesn't turn on impact.

By holding the club firmly, I don't mean squeezing it to death; that's unnecessary and unduly tightens up your swing. Hold the club only firmly enough to keep the clubhead under control. Having control of the club at all times is also what I meant a while ago when I talked about becoming "golf strong."

The first problem—straying off line—usually comes from a poor takeaway, which I would like to briefly discuss. One way to do this is to tell you what a bad takeaway is. It is sometimes called "picking up the club," and it is caused by impatience. The golfer is so anxious to swing at the ball that he puts the clubhead in motion with his hands. It is almost as though he were "jerking" the clubhead back from the ball.

By contrast, the good golfer has a feeling that he is moving the clubhead back from the ball smoothly. The pro golfer sometimes refers to a proper takeway as a "one piece" takeaway. By this he means that everything flows in unison—not only the hands, but with the hands the arms and body moving together in a single motion.

Tempo is another ingredient of a good swing. Another word for tempo is "speed"—how fast you want the clubhead to travel as it comes down through the ball.

If your chip shots are erratic—sometimes short of the mark and sometimes long—it is invariably because you do not have a

182

consistent tempo to your swing. You are probably guilty of the most common fault of the poor golfer—trying to gauge distance by hitting some shots "soft" and others "firmly," and often as not having doubts during your swing about how "hard" to hit the ball.

I believe you should hit every chip shot with the same tempo. Once you have a consistent tempo, all that is necessary to vary how far the ball travels in the air is to adjust the length of your backswing.

Developing a consistent tempo comes only from practice.

Here is one exercise for doing this. Practice swinging the club through a short chip shot, but without a golf ball. Keep repeating this exercise until you feel that each swing has the same tempo.

Next, take your stance and try the same swing, but this time with a golf ball. How far does the ball travel and where does it land? Now try another golf ball and repeat the exercise—always trying to take the clubhead back the same distance and swinging through the ball with the same tempo.

If you are doing this correctly, your shots should start showing consistency, falling increasingly into a pattern at, or near, the same spot on the green. You will be passing through the first stage of mastering the chip shot.

Next, you should move back a few yards. Keep the same tempo but lengthen your backswing just enough so that the ball again starts to land at or near your target. You have to be realistic about this process. You are not going to meet all of your chipping needs in one practice session. At this point there are many things that can affect your result. Our objective is to tackle the components of a good chip shot, one at a time.

For now, and for many of your early practice sessions, it is more important that you develop a consistent tempo than that you strike the ball the same way each time. That will come with time. This is not only a good rule now, but later. Even a proficient golfer occasionally loses his "touch" on his chip shots. When that happens, the first thing to check is your tempo. Go back to the practice area and repeat our exercise,

first without a golf ball and then with one. It will usually restore your short game.

Before we move on to another part of the chip shot, let's take still another look at "tempo." One question that high-handicap golfers often ask me is "how fast" they should swing the club. This is a matter of individual ability.

Again I can define the proper tempo by saying that poor tempo is when the clubhead moves more slowly than it should and the golfer has either a lazy swing or an overly deliberate one, or when the swing is so quick that it is rushed. The best way to judge the proper tempo for your game is to sense when the clubhead is under control at all times, moving quickly enough to make the swing feel free and easy, with the feeling that the club is firmly in your hands throughout the swing.

If you believe that you have the fundamentals of a chip shot firmly in mind, let's move on to discuss the three different styles of chip shot so you can decide which best suits your game.

The first type of a chip shot is made almost entirely with the hands. In this sense it breaks the rule about a one-piece takeaway. Your arms move hardly at all. As a matter of fact, some players keep their right arm against their body throughout the shot. The clubhead is swung back with the hands and, after the slightest of pauses, is swung back down again. The backswing is rarely, if ever, as much as waist high.

Only after the club has contacted the ball do your arms come into play to continue the clubhead forward and through the ball so that the clubhead stays low to the ground. Like the follow-through on any stroke, this is extremely important.

The follow-through "guarantees" that you have hit the ball properly. It also guards against any tendency to "quit" on a shot, and is a way to prevent the most common error in a chip shot.

Put this down in your "must remember" list; it applies to all methods of chip shots, including the hand-action version:

The biggest single error in a chip shot is trying to "scoop" the ball into the air.

It is the loft of the club that gets the ball airborne. You must hit the ball firmly and let the club do the work. Trying to "lift" the ball with your clubhead almost always results in a scuffed ball or a clubhead that buries itself in the ground behind the ball. Sometimes it results in missing the ball completely.

A second method of chipping—the punch shot—is for the more sophisticated golfer. This is the shot that the pro will use when he deliberately wants to hit a low-flying ball; for example, one that must go under tree branches, or one that must be hit low into the wind. In a punch shot, the clubface is "hooded"—the golfer makes it strike the ball with less than its normal amount of loft. This, in turn, produces a lower flying ball.

Here's how it's done. The clubhead is taken back low to the ground and exclusively with the hands and arms; there is no body pivot at all. The follow-through must also be low to the ground. The key to this shot is to keep the hands ahead of the clubhead at the instant of impact. This is in obvious contrast to the normal golf shot, in which the hands will be even with or slightly behind the ball at the point of impact.

As I said, the punch shot is a very valuable shot for the pro. It keeps the ball low and produces greater roll on the ball when it lands. But it requires a firm grip on the club, and the clubhead must be kept low upon the impact and follow-through.

The third method of chipping is the one that I prefer. It is essentially a "baby" version of the regular golf swing. There is some hand action, but only enough to put some "give" into the swing. I take the clubhead back from the ball with my wrists held firmly, until the momentum of the clubhead takes hold and "naturally" starts to cock my wrists. In other words, I don't consciously decide to cock my wrists; they become cocked from the movement of the clubhead.

We have already discussed the importance of establishing a constant tempo to the swing. For this reason I know that if I take the clubhead back a given distance on my backswing, my tempo will propel the ball a given distance to the green.

On very short chip shots my wrists will cock very little, probably not even noticeably to the spectator. As the distance I have to cover increases, my backswing will lengthen, and the cocking of my wrists will consequently become more pronounced. Whatever form of chip shot you decide is best suited for your game, the proper execution starts with a smooth takeaway. When you have mastered that, you're on your way toward the expert class in chipping. (See Illustration #9.)

The next essential to good chipping is your grip. High handicappers whose chip shots are erratic usually lose control of the club, which usually happens in two critical places.

The first is at the top of the backswing, just before starting the downswing. Many golfers instinctively loose their grip on the club at this point, tighten it for the downswing. Because the golfer doesn't consciously loosen and re-grip the club, this error is hard to spot.

It shows up pretty obviously in the results, however, because it takes the golf club out of control for a fraction of a second, which is enough to take the clubhead away from its square-to-the-target profile and cost the accuracy of the shot. One way to check on whether you are falling into this error is to pay attention to the ''feel'' of the club. If you have a sense that it is loose in your hands and that you are tightening up on the downswing, you may well be making this error.

You can also try to hold your swing at the top of your backswing and test how well you have the club under control.

The second place in which a golfer can lose control is at the moment of contact of the clubhead with the ball. Even if the clubhead returns squarely to the ball on impact, it will turn in your hands if your grip is not firm, and the ball will scoot off line, usually to the right of your objective.

As I have mentioned before, the follow-through is also important in checking on your swing. If the clubhead has been taken away properly and your downswing is correct, it will follow through on the straight path to the cup.

On the other hand, if the clubhead doesn't follow that path, you have strayed off line somewhere prior to contacting the

Illustration #9

ball. I usually have a follow-through that is roughly as long my backswing. This too serves a useful purpose. It means that my body is in balance throughout the golf swing.

If your body feels out of balance during your swing, step away from the ball and try your chip shot again without the ball. Then ask yourself these questions:

- Did I swing the club back smoothly?
- Did my wrists cock naturally?
- Was the club always firmly in my grip?
- Did the clubhead return squarely to the ball?
- Did my body move with the flow of the swing?
- Did I let the clubhead follow through without quitting on the stroke?

In the answers to these six questions you should be able to spot the source of your problem.

Chapter 13

Grooving Your Swing

Earlier in the book we talked about how to spot mental errors and how to correct them. Now let's talk about how to spot mechanical errors.

A good golfer should be a good diagnostician. He watches the action of the ball, and from it decides what caused it. Let's take the most common of all golfing problems—the slice. It has many causes, but all due to only three possible causes:

- A clubhead that is facing outward on impact.
- A clubhead that is technically square to the ball, but whose path is across the ball so that it imparts a slicing spin to the ball.
- A combination of the first two factors, with the clubhead facing outward and cutting across the ball.

One way to find out whether you are slicing is to watch where the ball lands when you hit your chip shots. If it has a tendency to land to the right side of where you aimed it, and if on landing it tends to drift to the right, you are almost certainly slicing the ball.

The first place to check in correcting this is your grip, because it is a frequent source of the problem.

It isn't easy to get a good grip on a golf club; and it is even tougher to change the one you have. I can tell you that from

personal experience. Tom Watson believes that my grip has always been my biggest handicap, and I'm inclined to agree.

I have a tendency to set my right hand too far left. I began that way, probably because I'm naturally left-handed. It took me a whole year to move my grip a quarter inch to the right. I do not believe there is such a thing as a standard grip for all persons. For example, while I have fairly good-sized hands, you may not. Your build, the angle of your swing, and many other things make each of us different golfers with different sets of needs.

Some golfers get good results with the so-called baseball grip, in which both hands grip the club. Bob Rosburg uses this grip. There are also a number of fine players who employ the interlocking grip, in which the little finger of the right hand interlocks with the forefinger of the left hand. This grip is often used by players who have small hands. Probably the most famous player who uses it is Jack Nicklaus.

Therefore, you should use the grip that seems best for you. Still, there is a model grip that is worth trying. If, after experimenting, you find that it doesn't work for you, you can change it to suit yourself.

Grasp the club shaft in your left hand. I usually leave about a half inch or an inch of the top of the shaft. Now put your thumb down along the center of the shaft.

Next put your right hand on the shaft, with the little finger overlapping the left index finger. The right thumb should lie across the center of the shaft.

The important thing is to grasp the club primarily in your fingers rather than in the palms of your hands. As I pointed out previously, it is essential to hold the club firmly, but not tightly. How do you know if you are gripping the club correctly? The best way is to check the Vs formed by your thumbs and forefingers. They should point to your right shoulder. (See Illustration #10.)

Another tip that I find helpful is to check my right hand. It should be square to the target. If your right hand is "open," or

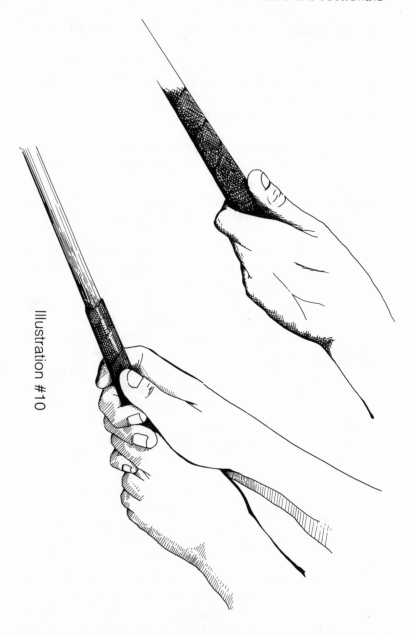

Illustration #10

if the Vs point too far past your right shoulder, you're inviting a slice.

Once you have settled on your grip, the next step is to get into position to swing the club. Most pro golfers have a little ritual that they go through when walking up to the ball. It helps to concentrate their thinking, but also eases their tension. Try it yourself.

Walk up to your ball from directly behind it and on the correct line to your objective. Then stop a few yards back from the ball, line up, and try your practice swing. This ritual doesn't happen to fit my style of play, but I know that it works for many golfers. It amounts to a "dress rehearsal" of the shot they are about to try.

If you don't use the practice-swing approach, go directly to the ball and place your clubhead right behind it and square to the target. Now glance up at the target and adjust your feet until you feel comfortably balanced. The purpose of setting your club behind the ball before planting your feet is to avoid a frequent error—reaching for the ball. That's what happens when you concentrate on foot position instead of the target.

Next you want to loosen up a bit, and for many golfers this means a "waggle." This loosens you up before settling down for your swing. One form of the waggle is to take your stance and place the clubhead behind the ball. Then, when your feet are set, lift the club and swing it back and forth over the ball, perhaps a foot or so in either direction. Now return the club to its proper position behind the ball.

What you have done is to establish yourself, loosen up your hands and body, and take a mini-swing. Other golfers waggle by lifting the clubhead above the ball and putting it back on the ground—being careful, of course, not to let the clubhead hit the ball.

Whether you waggle or not, or which waggle you use, isn't important. What is important is to feel comfortable in addressing the ball. And this means your weight must be evenly distributed. When you address the ball, you should not be leaning forward so that your weight is on your toes; nor should you

be standing so that your weight is on either your left or right foot. Instead, it should be evenly distributed.

The best way to achieve this is to bend your knees just slightly. This is often described as "sitting down" to the ball. Perhaps you can visualize the correct position if I say that it's like sitting on the edge of a bar stool.

Let me tell you why your setup is important. First, it is the base of your golf swing. You are going to swing a golf club back a considerable distance, stop momentarily, and then swing the club back down through the ball and complete your arc.

If you are going to swing with any kind of fluid motion, you must have the ability to shift your weight and maintain your balance throughout. If your knees are slightly bent, they provide some of the flexibility needed for this. (See Illustration #11.)

One more thing about your stance. There are three ways to address the ball. One is with the toes of both feet touching a line parallel to the direction to the cup. Golfers call this the "square" stance. Pulling your left foot back slightly from that parallel line creates an "open" stance. Pulling your right foot back from the line creates a "closed" stance.

This, too, is the source of a lot of unnecessary confusion. Some golfers with a tendency to slice believe they can cure it by resorting to an exaggerated closed stance. This sometimes works because the position of the feet can make a difference in the flight of the ball. A good player can fade or draw a ball by changing the position of his feet.

But his foot position works for him because he also has hand control at the point of impact, while the amateur does not. In the case of the high-handicap player, the extreme closed stance produces a ball with erratic flight that not infrequently flies straight, but far off to the right. Fortunately, there are better ways to cure a slice.

Let's take a look at what happens when the clubhead strikes the ball.

If the clubhead is turned outward on impact, the ball is naturally going to fly off to the right. If the clubhead is turned in-

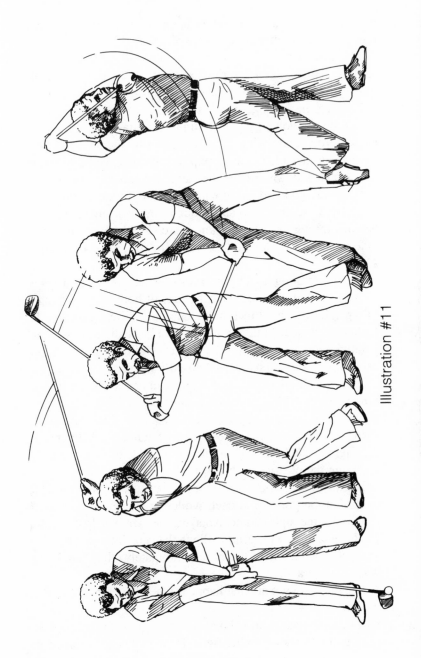

Illustration #11

ward, the ball will fly to the left. Even if the clubhead strikes the ball squarely, the ball will not necessarily travel straight to the target.

Whether the ball flies straight ahead will depend not only on the clubface being square to the target, but also on the direction in which the clubhead is traveling as it approaches the ball, strikes the ball, and follows through.

Think about this for a moment.

Let's put a golf club down on the ground in front of the ball as we did earlier in our lesson. The shaft of the club will represent the line to the cup. If the clubhead travels down that line and if it is square to the ball when it strikes the ball, the ball will travel straight.

Suppose that the clubhead doesn't travel straight down that line; that it comes from outside that line, strikes the ball, and then continues its path inside the line. You then have an "outside-in" swing. Even though the clubhead is square on impact, it is cutting across the ball. It puts a clockwise spin on the ball and creates the classic slice.

When you combine two faults—the outside-in path of the clubhead and a clubhead that is turned slightly outward on impact—you have something else: an even bigger slice. But while this is a problem, it also provides the basis for an answer. If you are going to get rid of a chronic slice, you first have got to control your grip so that the clubhead makes contact squarely with the ball. Then you must make sure the clubhead doesn't travel through the hitting area on an outside-in path.

Some golfers control the clubhead so that it travels from inside the line to the pin and, after impact, follows through outside the line. This is the inside-out swing, which tends to produce a hooking ball. A hook is usually superior to a ball that slices, but it can still give the golfer a fair number of headaches.

The best swing for most golfers is an inside-inside swing in which the clubhead approaches the ball from inside the line to the cup, strikes the ball, and on the follow-through stays inside the line.

Fine, you say, but how do I do that? It may sound facetious, but the way to do it right is not to do it wrong. So, let's see if we can get rid of the tendencies that produce the wrong line to the pin—the golfing faults that cause the outside-in swing. The first place to look for error is in the takeaway.

A bad takeaway is often the problem. It destroys your aim and is likely to throw your clubhead outside the line. As we pointed out earlier, the cure for this is to develop a smooth, even, takeaway.

The second place to look for trouble is at the top of the backswing. This is the point where a loose grip can cost control of the club. It is also where the golfer can rush the start of his downswing, or where he can start the clubhead back incorrectly and throw it out of line.

The third culprit is poor weight distribution. In my experience, this is a prime reason for a slice and a history of haphazard results off the tee.

Here is what happens. The golfer sets up with his weight primarily on his left side, but then leaves it there during his backswing. As a result several things have to happen—none of them good.

In order to maintain his balance he has to lean to the left during his backswing, and then lean back to his right on the downswing. He loses power, balance, and rhythm, and can only bring the club back down by throwing it outside its proper arc.

On the other hand, the golfer who sets up with his weight mainly on his right foot (the so-called "reverse" pivot) also has nothing but trouble. He really can't pivot, so he is prone to slapping the ball, sometimes even missing it completely. If he does take a full backswing, he will invariably sway to the left on his downswing.

It isn't just the amateur who has a problem with weight distribution; it can sometimes be a pro as well, but for a slightly different reason. Almost every pro starts out correctly, weight balanced, but some have difficulty moving their weight to their right side on the backswing.

The problem is usually traceable to a golfer's failure to turn his shoulders properly. Jack Nicklaus found an interesting way to overcome that problem. As he addresses the ball, he cocks his head to the right so that he is looking at the back of the ball with his left eye. This puts his head in a position where it won't move during his shoulder turn.

Many golfers, however, never learn to manage. One was Bob Menne. Bob joined the tour in 1970, and he had only moderate success until the 1974 Kemper Open at Quail Hollow in Charlotte, North Carolina. Jerry Heard had already completed his round. Bob was coming into the 18th hole and he needed a birdie to force a playoff.

What happened was one of the great pressure putts I can remember. Bob Menne put his approach shot on the green and had about a ten-foot putt to the pin. That's pressure enough. But there was something else. Another player in his foursome was J.C. Snead and his ball was just a bit farther away from the cup which meant he putted first.

Snead was out of contention, but instead of taking his usual stance and putting away, he proceeded to take his time, measuring and re-measuring, setting up and stepping back. It took several minutes before he finally putted his ball.

Snead was a close friend of Jerry Heard and it looked as though he was delaying so it would build up pressure on Menne. This is not unlike a pro football game in which the opposing team calls timeout before the other team tries a field goal in order to put pressure on the kicker.

In this case, it didn't work. Not only did Menne sink that putt, but he went on the next day to win the playoff with Heard. But even that victory underscored a basic weakness in Menne's game. He was great around the greens, but he had a fatal flaw in his long irons and woods. As he began his backswing, his head would drop and interfere with his shoulder turn. As a result his weight failed to shift and his swing was erratic.

I've mentioned before that a pro will often seek the help of another pro when he has a problem he can't solve himself. Right after he won the Kemper, Menne went to Alabama to

work with one of the great teacher-pros, Jim Ballard, who tried his best to break Menne's habit of dropping his head. But after a week, they gave up.

Said Bob sadly, "There are some dogs who just won't learn not to chase cars."

It is true that it is hard to break old habits, but I think you can learn the proper swing if you understand what happens when you start out with your weight on one side and leave it there during the backswing. What happens in each of these cases is that the clubhead follows a different arc with each swing. The new arc is invariably outside the correct arc, and it is impossible to get back inside before striking the ball.

The knack of developing a consistent inside-inside swing is to begin properly. This begins with a good stance. I favor a square stance for most golfers or, at most, a slightly closed stance with the right foot drawn back about an inch from the line to the cup. I also like the ball to be slightly to the left of the middle of my stance.

The rest of the swing boils down to concentrating on a few particulars. Get yourself in good balance right from dhe start. Then move the clubhead back smoothly on the backswing, with your grip firm but not viselike.

Keep your backswing rhythmic and smooth. Bring the clubhead down and through the ball and don't stop until you have completed a smooth follow-through.

The best way to judge whether you have hit the ball correctly or not is from the flight of the ball. But there are other ways to tell. If your swing is in the proper groove, you should wind up still feeling well balanced on your feet. Your hands should be high, holding the club firmly in the follow-through. Most important, you should have heard the satisfying crack of the ball on impact. Then you know you are on the way to better golf.

One of the popular sayings in business is the KISS theory. The letters stand for "Keep It Simple, Stupid." Well, it applies to golf, but in a different way. I recommend the idea to "Keep It Simple" and if you do, you'll find it's not stupid; it is being smart.

It is possible to make golf a highly technical game, and a lot of people try to do this. Some instructors tell you to vary your stance, the position of the ball, or the tempo of your swing. Others tell you how to pivot, turn your shoulders, or place your hands. You name it, they somehow connect it with your golf swing.

There are those who say "keep your head still." But if you keep your head down deliberately, it can tie up your swing. Two of the best golfers, Tom Weiskopf and Ben Crenshaw, both move their heads about six or seven inches as the club goes back.

Other people tell you to bring the club back down in the same plane as your backswing, which you simply can't do because your shoulders turn horizontally. As Claude Harmon once remarked, the only way you can come up and down in the same plane is when you're flying to Miami.

I think one of the reasons it is so hard for the high handicapper to break his bad golf habits is that he makes golf too complicated. Rather than setting up a whole bunch of do's-and-don'ts, the best way to get your game under control is to keep your golf as simple as possible. The fewer things you have to concern yourself with, the fewer things there are to go wrong.

As a matter of fact, I believe you really start to become a good golfer when you stop thinking about everything except where you want the ball to go.

Let's start right now to eliminate as many variables as possible.

First, I think you should always tee up the ball at the same height whether you're hitting a drive or a 9-iron off the tee.

Second, keep the same swing with every club. Once you've warmed up with a short iron, you should be ready to take any club, up to and including the long woods, without having to alter your swing. The only difference in these clubs is in the extension: how far away the ball is from you.

The only other thing that changes is your stance due to the length of the club you use. In order to maintain good balance,

most golfers will open up their stance somewhat as they move into the 7-, 8-, and 9-irons. This makes it easier to keep the clubface square.

On the other hand, the takeaway—although shorter—is the same. If you are trying a short chip shot, your backswing won't be as long as it would be if you were hitting off the tee; nor will your follow-through extend as far.

The key parts of the swing, however, won't change. You still need to hit down and through the ball with every club. You need to bring the clubhead squarely to the ball and on an inside-inside path. And you still need to strive for a smooth, even swing. Changing clubs doesn't change the need to properly execute each of the essentials of a good swing.

The mark of the experienced golfer is that he uses every club in the bag. According to the rules, you may carry fourteen clubs, but not everybody carries the same set. A pro, for example, may elect to carry a 1-iron if he feels it will give him greater control off the tee. An amateur will rarely use that club.

It is up to you to choose your clubs, depending on your game and the course you are going to play. Your selection also has to be based on common sense.

Because of the limitation on the number of clubs you may carry, it doesn't make sense to carry a club you don't use at the expense of one that would prove more useful. But it also doesn't make sense to carry a club in your bag if you don't know how to use it properly.

The right idea is to master all the clubs in your bag. And the best way to master all of them is to start by mastering a few. Specifically, I suggest starting out with four clubs:

- A 3- or 4-wood
- A 5-iron
- A sand wedge
- A putter

You will use the 3- or 4-wood for driving and for long fairway shots, the 5-iron for mid-range and pitch-and-run shots,

the wedge for short iron shots, including sand bunker shots and, of course, you will use your putter on the greens.

Leave the rest of your clubs home and try playing with just these four. It stands to reason that you won't score as well because you won't have a full range of clubs.

What you will have, however, are the essential tools for playing golf. If you can control these four clubs, the rest will come easy. As a matter of fact, the rest will come easier because you will have learned another secret of the pros—the ability to "finesse" a shot.

Because you simply won't have the versatility with these four clubs that you would with a full bag of clubs you can also learn another invaluable lesson: How to substitute position for power.

This means making up distance by placing the ball more expertly on each shot.

In order to play a round of golf with just four clubs, you have to start out by judging how far you hit with each. Let's say you hit a 3-wood about 180 yards, a 5-iron 150 yards, and a sand wedge 90 yards.

What do you do if the distance to the green is somewhere between that for a 3-wood and a 5-iron? The answer is to hit the 3-wood but not the full distance. The same concept would follow if you had a 135-yard shot that fell between the range of your 5-iron and your sand wedge.

You've got to "take something off" your normal distance.

The best way to shorten up your distance with any club is to do three things:

1. Choke down on the club.
2. Shorten your backswing.
3. Never shorten your follow-through.

We discussed gripping down on the club when we talked about the chip shot. As you recall, it simply meant moving your grip further down the club; instead of just exposing a half

inch or so of the grip, move your hands down until a couple of inches are exposed.

Among other things, you will find that you have greater confidence when you grip down. You know you have enough club in your hands to hit the shot you're facing, and there is no temptation to go all out. Also, by shortening your backswing, you have just a little more control over the club.

It is essential to remember a point I made earlier: The one thing you should not change is the tempo of your swing. Even when you grip down and shorten your backswing you should keep a consistent swing through all of your clubs. A constant tempo is the only way to develop consistency in your game.

It will take experience to judge just how much to shorten your swing. I suggest you experiment with a quarter swing, half swing, and a three-quarter swing and determine just how far each carries the ball. Once you've learned these variations, you have, in effect, added a whole series of new shots to your repertoire, and greatly expanded your alternatives.

One place where you will find this most helpful is in your short game. As you get close to the green, you have two options. The first of these is the chip shot—the low flying ball that hits and runs toward the pin—which I recommend using whenever you are less than twenty-five yards from the green.

Sometimes you don't have enough green; if you hit the ball onto the putting surface, it will roll too far. In that case, if there are no intervening traps, you can still use the chip shot by aiming for the fringe in front of the green and letting the grass slow the ball down.

I use the grass as a "brake" only when I have to; whenever I can, I aim for the green itself. Sometimes, however, you don't have an option; there may be a trap between your ball and the green, and you have to pitch the ball into the air to clear it.

Your second option is the pitch shot, which is preferable when you are more than twenty-five yards from the green. A pitch shot produces a high-flying ball with backspin, and from farther out it gives you better control of the ball.

In our four-club project, the sand wedge becomes our club

for the pitch shot. If a full swing with a sand wedge produces a ninety-yard shot, we can apply the grip-down idea and the shortened swing to give us the desired shorter shot. Again, remind yourself to maintain the regular tempo you use with your other shots.

When you go to your full fourteen-club game, you can obviously pinpoint your distances even more closely; for example, you have an option between a full 6-iron shot and a gripped-down 5-iron shot.

Let me remind you briefly about your stance. I believe most golfers should use the square stance with their woods and with their irons down through the 6-iron.

For the shorter irons (the 7-iron, 8-iron, 9-iron, and sand or pitching wedge) it is desirable to open up your stance slightly by bringing your left foot back somewhat from the line to the pin.

You should also shorten the distance between your feet as the clubs become more lofted.

Chapter 14

Getting Out of Sand Traps

There is one other shot with the short irons, and it requires special techniques. That is the explosion shot to get your ball out of a sand trap. You don't always have to "explode" out of a sand trap, but it becomes the only effective shot you can try if the ball is buried in the sand.

Earlier in this chapter I said that you hit all shots in golf the same way. There is one exception. The explosion shot is the only shot that is really different from all the rest. It is the shot to use when your ball is partly, or fully, buried in the sand. With it, you have to try to hit the ball with an open clubface. It also differs from every other shot in golf in that you hit the sand first. It is the force of the sand against the ball that forces it to "pop" out.

Probably the two greatest difficulties for beginners are water hazards and sand trap shots. Both are largely mental problems which take practice and experience to overcome.

There are several reasons why sand shots are troublesome, at least for the amateur. Not only do you hit the ball with the clubface open, but under the rules you are not allowed to "ground" your club in the sand.

So, unlike the case with other clubs whose clubheads you can put down on the ground in back of the ball and get set up, you have to use a combination of imagination and judgment in preparing for a wedge shot out of the sand.

There is another reason why sand traps give amateurs difficulty: Very few golfers practice bunker shots. They depend on luck to keep them out of traps, and when they land in one they have little experience to guide them.

There are times when you will be in a trap in a position that is level with the fringe of the green, and can escape with your putter.

But if you are in a trap with a high lip, or if your ball is partly buried, the explosion shot is the proper tactic.

There is also a tendency to slice from the trap. One thing that seems to help many golfers avoid the slice is to take as long a hold on the sand wedge as possible, grabbing it near the end of the shaft. Bend your knees more than usual.

Let's see how to do it. The first essential is to get a firm footing. I take a slightly wider stance than usual and wiggle my feet in the sand until I feel I have a good grip with my spikes.

What we are going to do is use a "cut" shot, in which the clubhead "cuts" under the ball. We want to lay the clubface back so that it is open, and we want the clubhead to come from the outside to the inside.

The best way to accomplish this is to stand so that you are turned partway toward the target. I'd estimate this turn to be about 30 degrees. This gives you a more open stance. Play the ball just off your left heel, and as you get set up, make sure the clubhead is open. (See Illustration #12.)

Aim just behind the ball and, as with every stroke, strike a descending blow. I use about a three-quarter swing and aim about an inch or so in back of the ball. It is important to have a firm grip so the clubhead doesn't stop. You must follow through for this shot to be effective. There is one exception. If the ball is buried in the sand—pros call it the "fried egg" position—the correct way is to hit down into the sand and let the sand "explode" the ball out onto the green. For the buried shot, don't follow through.

Although in our four-club practice session the sand wedge is your club for escaping the sand trap, you may sometimes want to use an 8-iron, 9-iron or, occasionally, a pitching wedge when playing with a full set of clubs.

Illustration #12

The sand wedge has a heavy flange that enables it to do its work. The pitching wedge is similar but somewhat lighter, and doesn't have quite as much loft. One of the times when you might want to switch to the pitching wedge is when there is no lip on the trap and you have a favorable lie.

On the other hand, you may want to discard your pitching wedge and substitute the sand wedge when you are caught in heavy rough, and the extra weight and heavier flange help give your shot the needed momentum.

The "cut" shot can be used elsewhere on the golf course when you need more than the usual amount of backspin. One example would be in a 100-yard approach shot to a green on which the pin is near the front edge and the run with a normal shot would carry your ball too far.

The cut shot is also an effective technique when your ball is buried in deep rough. With this shot, the ball tends to rise quickly and with extra height, which makes it useful in clearing a tree or clump of bushes in your path to the green.

I will warn you in advance, however, that this is a difficult shot to master and takes plenty of practice. But if you are willing to work your way into the expert-golfer category, the cut shot is a valuable addition to your game.

You can take your stance as I suggested for the explosion shot, turning partway toward your target and opening up the clubface.

However, there is another way to achieve the same setup, which some golfers find easier and which gives the same results.

Take your regular stance with an 8-iron, 9-iron, or wedge, with the clubface square to the target. Now shift the club so that it points slightly to the right of the target. Then regrip the club.

Now turn your body enough so that your clubface is once more square to the ball. What you have done is to "open up" your stance so that you are facing more directly at your target. This also helps guarantee that the clubhead will travel the outside-inside path, which in this case is the proper one.

The key to this shot is to keep the clubface laid back so that the club slices under the ball. It also requires that your hands be "active" and your grip firmly on the club shaft.

There are four other shots that you must master in order to round out your game—the uphill, downhill, and two kinds of sidehill lies. Even if all of your shots stayed in the fairway, you would still, on many occasions, have a tough lie. The ground, even on the fairway, isn't always level, and any time you are shooting from an uneven lie you have lost the natural balance you have on level ground.

In my judgment, the most difficult of the four shots named above is the downhill lie. Your weight will be more on your left side than evenly balanced. Your swing is impeded, and you don't have as clear a view of the ball as you would on level ground. I find it helpful to try a few practice swings to get accustomed to the uneven lie. It is also a good idea to play the ball more to your right than usual, and to take a club one or even two numbers higher (more lofted) than you would for the same distance from a level lie.

There is a tendency to fade to the right on a downhill lie. One way to compensate for this is to aim somewhat to the left of your target. It is important to avoid chopping down at the ball or, worse, hitting the ground behind the ball. This is usually caused by the golfer trying to "help" the ball into the air by scooping at it instead of letting the loft of the club do its work.

One other tip: Cut down the length of your backswing. This helps keep your swing under control—which is important in all of your shotmaking, but especially important in your "trouble" shooting.

The uphill lie requires a different approach than does the downhill lie. When you are shooting from an uphill lie, the ball takes a higher trajectory, and you should therefore cut back one or two clubs to one with a less lofted clubface. Also, because this shot tends to pull to the left, you should aim somewhat to the right of your target.

Again, shorten your backswing for greater control.

Neither an uphill nor a downhill lie is usually very comfortable, but one of the most awkward shots in golf occurs with a sidehill lie in which the ball is lower than your feet. The ball seems a long way off and you can fall easily into the bad habit of "reaching" for it.

There is also a tendency to slice from this position. One thing that seems to help many golfers with this shot is to take as long a hold on the club as possible, grabbing it near the end of the shaft. You should also bend your knees more than usual and be sure to keep your clubhead down at the level of the ball throughout the swing to avoid topping the ball.

With a sidehill lie in which the ball is higher than your feet, you can adjust by gripping down on the club, using a shorter backswing, and keeping your weight more on the balls of your feet.

With all four of these bad lies, concentrate on your balance and give a special effort to making good contact with the ball. And follow through; don't quit on the shot. That's good advice anywhere on the golf course, but is especially true when a poor lie takes away your natural swing.

Chapter 15

Setting Your Goals

We've spent some time together, you and I, talking about golf. I've given you my philosophy of the game—what I think is important to know and do if you are serious about playing better golf.

In these closing pages, let me try to summarize the key points.

1. The most effective way to improve quickly is to THINK SMART GOLF.
2. There is no substitute for practice, but it must be fundamentally sound practice. Too many golfers simply practice their mistakes.
3. Prepare before you tee off. Warm up with your long clubs but allow some practice time on the putting green.
4. If you are in trouble anywhere on the course, make it your number-one priority to get out of trouble and onto the fairway or putting green.
5. Try to avoid making two mistakes in a row.
6. Master the short game and your putting. The quality of your golf depends on how well you play in the distance from 100 yards out and when you're near the cup.
7. Study your game. Find the places where errors are hurting it, and seek solutions.
8. Set realistic goals for improvement.

I think it is helpful for any golfer to set a series of goals for his game. You must set standards for yourself and strive to meet them if you are going to progress.

If you are a scratch golfer, here are some guidelines:

1. You should be able to score a par-3 on any hole up to 160 yards long.
2. You should strive to score par on any par-4 hole up to 390 yards long.
3. You should get down in five strokes on any hole under 595 yards long.
4. On any par hole longer than those above, you should get down in par at least half the time.
5. Whenever you are within twenty-five feet of the cup, you should be able to get down in two strokes.

If you are a golfer who shoots in the 80s, you should make it a goal to accomplish the following:

1. Drive 200 yards consistently and average 190 yards on your second shot.
2. If you are within 100 yards of the green, be able to put your approach shot within fifteen feet of the cup.
3. Take no more than two putts any time you are within fifteen feet of the cup.
4. Sink every putt if it is a foot or less from the cup.

The 90 shooter should average 180 yards on his tee shots, woods, and long irons. This enables him to afford a "safety" shot when needed to get the ball back on the fairway.

If you are a 90 shooter, here are some other guidelines:

1. From 150 yards, you should hole out in four strokes or less.
2. From twenty-five to thirty yards off the green, you

should be able to put the ball within about ten feet of the cup.

3. From ten feet away, you should invariably take no more than two putts.

What about the 100+ shooter?

1. He should try to have no more than one 6 on any par-3 hole.
2. He should avoid more than one 7 on any par-4 hole.
3. He should never have more than one 8 on any par-5 hole.
4. How does this golfer reach those goals? First, he should work on putting, with the objective of never taking more than three putts on any green.
5. Next, he should develop his short game, with a view to always getting the ball into the cup with no more than four strokes if the ball is within ninety yards of the green.
6. If he is in a trap or in the rough, he should never take more than two strokes to get back onto either the fairway or the green.

None of these goals is easy, but each is worth striving for. Once you reach one set of goals, try for the next.

As a final word, I can do no better than repeat the advice of one of the all-time great competitors, Jimmy Demaret, who said that the secret of golf was to play it one shot at a time, to which I might add: to play each shot the best way you know how.